At Issue

What Limits Should Be Placed on Presidential Powers?

Other Books in the At Issue Series:

At Issue

What Limits Should Be Placed on Presidential Powers?

Tamara L. Roleff, Book Editor

GREENHAVEN PRESS

An imprint of Thomson Gale, a part of The Thomson Corporation

THOMSON

™

GALE

Detroit • New York • San Francisco • New Haven, Conn. • Waterville, Maine • London

Christine Nasso, *Publisher*
Elizabeth Des Chenes, *Managing Editor*

© 2007 Thomson Gale, a part of The Thomson Corporation.

Thomson and Star logo are trademarks and Gale and Greenhaven Press are registered trademarks used herein under license.

For more information, contact:
Greenhaven Press
27500 Drake Rd.
Farmington Hills, MI 48331-3535
Or you can visit our Internet site at http://www.gale.com

LIBRARY OF CONGRESS CATALOGING-IN-PUBLICATION DATA

What limits should be placed on presidential powers? / Tamara L. Roleff, book editor.
    p. cm. -- (At issue)
    Includes bibliographical references and index.
    ISBN-13: 978-0-7377-3629-8 (lib. : alk. paper)
    ISBN-10: 0-7377-3629-1 (lib. : alk. paper)
    ISBN-13: 978-0-7377-3630-4 (pbk. : alk. paper)
    ISBN-10: 0-7377-3630-5 (pbk. : alk. paper)
    1. Executive power--United States. 2. Presidents--United States. 3. War on Terrorism, 2001– 4. War and emergency powers--United States. I. Roleff, Tamara L., 1959–
    KF5053.W43 2006
    342.73'06--dc22

                                                                    2006022969

Printed in the United States of America
10 9 8 7 6 5 4 3 2 1

Contents

Introduction

The U.S. Constitution outlines a separation of powers among the legislative, executive, and judiciary branches of the federal government, integrating checks and balances that prevent any branch from abusing its powers or violating constitutional principles or citizens' rights. The three branches and their responsibilities are traditionally viewed as separate but equal.

Several presidents, however, have argued that the constitutional division of federal power is not strictly balanced but hierarchical, with the president as the head of the government, a controversial position known as the unitary executive theory. The theory is based on two clauses of Article II of the Constitution, the so-called Vesting Clause and Take Care Clause, which state that "the executive power shall be vested in a President of the United States" and that the president "shall take care that the laws are faithfully executed."

Supporters of the unitary executive theory interpret these clauses broadly, maintaining, for example, that the president may not only veto a law passed by Congress but has the authority to determine how to implement the laws he signs. One way for the president to signal his intentions for implementing a new law is to issue a so-called signing statement when he signs the bill into law, indicating his interpretation of the law and how it will be executed. James Monroe (1817–1825) is credited with originating the signing statement, but until Ronald Reagan's presidency (1981–1989), only 75 signing statements had been issued in the previous two hundred years. Reagan and immediate successors George H.W. Bush and Bill Clinton together issued a total of 247 signing statements, but this increase in the practice drew little public attention. Scrutiny of signing statements tends to be most acute during national crises, especially wartime, and indeed controversy broke out in 2006, when reports focused attention on President George W. Bush's record of issuing more than 500 signing statements since taking office in 2001.

The statements that have sparked the most controversy are not those laying out the president's interpretation of the law he has just signed, but those asserting or implying the president's authority *not* to execute or adhere to provisions he believes conflict with his own duties as president and commander in chief. By signing the bill the president avoids antagonizing Congress with a veto, but such signing statements, some political analysts argue, actually nullify legislative acts, expand the president's powers, and put him above the law. Heated debate about the nature and limitation of executive power has followed.

One of Bush's most controversial signing statements was that issued with the McCain Detainee Amendment, a bill sponsored by Arizona senator John McCain, who was held prisoner and tortured by the North Vietnamese during the Vietnam War. Congress passed the amendment, which prohibits the torture of prisoners of war, including alleged terrorist detainees held at the military base in Guantanamo Bay, Cuba, and Bush signed it into law in December 2005. However, in his signing statement the president stated that the executive branch will construe the law in a manner consistent with his constitutional authority, and broad powers as president and commander in chief of the country's armed forces, to protect Americans from future terrorist attacks. Legal analysts have interpreted this wording as the president's assertion that if an act of Congress prohibiting the cruel, inhumane and degrading treatment of a detainee intrudes on the inherent power of the president to conduct the war on terrorism, he may disregard the law and authorize torture. Critics call this an abuse of power; supporters believe the president indeed is justified in waiving restrictions in the interest of national security.

About the same time as Bush's interpretation of the ban on torture was called into question, the *New York Times* broke the story that as far back as 2001 the president had covertly authorized the National Security Agency to eavesdrop on communications between U.S. residents and suspected terrorists without a warrant, a violation of the Foreign Intelligence Surveillance Act of 1978 (FISA). FISA requires that all surveillance on U.S. residents be approved by a special court set up just for that purpose. Of the nearly twenty-one thousand warrant applications for eavesdropping submitted since 1979, only four have been rejected by the FISA court, a record that critics of the covert program point to as evidence that obtaining a warrant is not a difficult or adversarial procedure.

Challenges to the covert program focused on Americans' right to privacy; the legality of eavesdropping on U.S. residents without a warrant; the number of Americans who had been spied on; the results of the eavesdropping; the effect of exposing the secret activity on national security; the legality of publicizing information about the classified program; and whether the president has the power to authorize such a surveillance program. The president defended his actions by again stressing his responsibility as commander in chief to do whatever is necessary to protect the security of the United States. He briefed members of Congress on the program and, he maintains, he and his advisers review the program every forty-five days to ensure American civil liberties are not being abused. In his defense of the program, Bush said, "If there are people inside our country who are talking with Al-Qaeda, we want to know about it."

Some evidence indicates that most Americans support these presidential efforts in the war on terrorism. An ABC News/*Washington Post* poll, taken in May 2006 following news reports that the National Security Agency was collecting the domestic phone records of millions of Americans, found that 63 percent of respondents considered this an acceptable way for the federal government to investigate terrorism. Sixty-five percent of respondents thought it was more important for the government to investigate possible terrorism than to protect the privacy of its citizens. Moreover, 66 percent said it would not bother them if the government had a record of their phone calls.

The contributors to *At Issue: What Limits Should Be Placed on Presidential Powers?* debate such timely issues as whether the president's signing statements, authorization of governmental eavesdropping without a warrant, and detainment of suspected terrorists are an abuse of power and violations of individual rights or are within the scope of the chief executive's constitutional duty to protect national security.

1

All Federal Executive Power
Is Vested in the President

Samuel A. Alito Jr.

Samuel A. Alito Jr. is an associate justice of the U.S. Supreme Court. Nominated to the Court by President George W. Bush in November 2005, Alito served under President Ronald Reagan from 1985–1987 as deputy assistant attorney general in the Office of Legal Counsel, where he provided constitutional advice for the executive branch.

The Framers of the U.S. Constitution deliberately chose a unitary executive (the president) rather than a plural executive (such as a cabinet or privy council) to lead the executive branch of government because they believed good government depended on an energetic, strong executive whose authority was not diffused or weakened by administrative dissension. Indeed, Article II of the Constitution explicitly vests executive-branch power in no one but the president. The president's duty, as head of the executive branch, is to faithfully execute, and supervise the execution of, U.S. law in the broad interest of all U.S. citizens; only the vigorous exercise of executive power can balance the power of Congress, in which opposing factions tend to protect narrow constituencies.

In the 13 years since I left OLC [Justice Department Office of Legal Counsel, in 1987] I have not had much occasion in my day-to-day work to think about the constitutional powers

Samuel A. Alito Jr., "Administrative Law and Regulation: Presidential Oversight and the Administrative State," *Engage: The Journal of the Federalist Society's Practice Groups*, vol. 2, pp. 11–13, November 2001. Reproduced by permission.

of the Presidency. But one case implicating the President's constitutional powers did come before me, and it may have some symbolic significance. The case involved a lawyer in Western Pennsylvania who had accumulated a number of parking tickets. He went to the mayor's office to complain about this, and he ended up being arrested for disorderly conduct. He was taken before a judge, the judge found him guilty, sentenced him to 90 days in jail, and to boot ordered that he undergo a psychiatric evaluation.

When this examination was conducted, one of the questions that was asked, believe it or not, was what he would do if he were the President of the United States. In a lawyerly fashion, he responded that he would carry out the duties of the office in accordance with the Constitution. This answer was interpreted as a sign of some mental instability. This is a true story. And he ended up being civilly committed and had considerable difficulty getting himself out of that situation. So obviously, it is dangerous at times in our society to think about the presidency in strictly constitutional terms.

The President has not just some executive powers, but the executive power—the whole thing.

When I was in OLC, however, we were known, actually, to read the text of the Constitution, in particular Article Two, as well as *The Federalist Papers*. We were strong proponents of the theory of the unitary executive, that all federal executive power is vested by the Constitution in the President. And I thought then, and I still think, that this theory best captures the meaning of the Constitution's text and structure, and that's what I want to talk about. For those of you who are very familiar with this argument, I will apologize to you in advance for preaching the gospel according to OLC in very simplified terms for at least a few minutes.

The Executive Branch

Let me begin with what is most rudimentary. In our constitutional sophistication we really shouldn't lose track of the most basic basics. And, if you read the Constitution, you will see as we all learned back in grade school, that the Constitution speaks of only three types of federal governmental power. Legislative, Executive, and Judicial. And it creates three corresponding branches of government: Legislative, Executive, and Judicial.

There is no mention in the Constitution of any fourth type of power, such as the administrative power, to which some very distinguished scholars have recently referred, or any fourth branch of government. So, if the administrative agencies are in the federal government, which they certainly are, they have to be in one of those branches, and the logical candidate is the executive branch.

Article II, Section One, makes the President the head of the executive branch, but it does more than that. It provides that "[t]he Executive Power shall be vested in a President of the United States." Thus, the President has not just some executive powers, but *the* executive power—the whole thing.

The language of Article II, Section One, stands in contrast with the similar, but in some respects, notably different language of Article III, which, of course, begins by saying that "[t]he Judicial Power of the United States shall be vested in one Supreme Court and in such inferior courts as Congress shall from time to time ordain and establish." Article II does not say the executive power shall be vested in a President of the United States and in such inferior executive departments or officers as the Congress shall from time to time ordain and establish. And the Founders certainly understood that there would be such inferior executive departments and officers. They're referred to elsewhere in the Constitution itself. They were created by the first Congress, but no part of the executive power was vested in them. The inference seems pretty compelling that the executive powers is vested in the President alone.

Now, what the executive power encompasses has been very hotly debated. But, at a minimum, it must mean the power to execute the law. If that's not apparent from the very phrase, "the executive power," Article II, Section Three, of course, provides that "the President shall take Care that the Laws be faithfully executed." Thus, the President has the power and the duty to supervise the way in which subordinate Executive Branch officials exercise the President's power of carrying federal law into execution.

The unitary executive [is] necessary to balance the huge power of the legislature and the factions that may gain control of it.

A Unitary Executive

The Constitutional Convention rejected the concept of a plural executive in favor of a unitary executive and it's important to recall why it did that. First, as Hamilton said in *Federalist 70*, the Framers wanted "energy in the executive." They wanted a vigorous executive, which they believed was important for good government in general, and for "the steady administration of the laws" in particular.

When executive power is diffused, Hamilton wrote, "the most bitter dissensions are apt to spring. And these will lessen the respectability, weaken the authority, and distract the plans and operations of government."

The Framers also saw the unitary executive as necessary to balance the huge power of the legislature and the factions that may gain contol of it.

And, finally, they wanted accountability. A divided executive, *Federalist 70* says, "tends to conceal faults and destroy responsibility." Now it's striking to me that these objectives are, if anything, more important today than they were at the time of the founding, when we had of course, a very small federal government.

The case for a unitary executive seems, if anything, stronger today than it was in the 18th Century.

Take energy. Obviously, with the vast nature of the federal establishment, a vigorous executive is needed for coordination. A vigorous executive is also needed to get anything done. It can be used to accomplish things that most probably would not favor. But, it's also necessary to reform existing programs, and it is necessary to restrain unwarranted and inefficient regulation.

The same is true for accountability. As we all know, Congress has taken to enacting statutes that leave it up to the administrative agencies to make many of the most important policy choices. So, Congress as an institution has abdicated its responsibility for those decisions when they are ultimately made. If the President takes the responsibility for supervising the agencies, then their decisions will be accountable through him to the electorate.

And finally, close presidential control of the executive tends to control factions. It's much easier for a faction to influence key elements in Congress, and those elements may see it as their best strategy to deliver as much as they can to their narrow constituencies. A President is generally responsible to a much broader electorate. So, for all of these reasons, the case for a unitary executive seems, if anything, stronger today than it was in the 18th Century.

As we all know, however, the Supreme Court has not exactly adopted the theory of the unitary executive. Instead (to try to simplify a great many cases) it seems to have taken something of the two-track approach.

When the Court has been confronted with something that seems to fall within a very specific provision of the Constitution, like the Appointments Clause, or the Presentment Clause, it has taken a rather strict approach. But when it's been confronted with an inroad on the general grant of executive power to the President, it has basically engaged in balancing.

Now what does this approach mean for restrictions on the President's ability to oversee the work of the administrative agencies? There are a few restrictions one might imagine that might fall within one of these specific textual provisions as the Supreme Court sees them—for example, a restriction on the President's ability to obtain information might be seen as falling within the clause that authorizes the President to require an opinion in writing from the principal officer of an executive department. But for the most part, the restrictions are probably going to be tested under some sort of balancing test, either one of the tests set out in *Morrison v. Olson*, or maybe in some instances the test for executive privilege.

The Independent Counsel Act

So in the few minutes remaining, I want to talk a little bit about *Morrison. Morrison*, of course, concerned the constitutionality of the late, but probably not very much lamented, Independent Counsel Act. Under the theory of the unitary executive, the contitutionality of this Act was questionable. But the Supreme Court, as we know, didn't see it that way, by vote of 7-1.

Upholding the Act's restriction on the ability of the Attorney general to remove an Independent Counsel, the Court said that such a restriction is permissible if it does not "impede the President's ability to perform his constitutional duty." In a similar vein, on the broader issue of whether the Act violated Article II as a whole, the Court said that the critical questions were whether the Act impermissibly undermined the powers of the Executive or "prevented the Executive from accomplishing its constitutionally assigned functions."

This is obviously very elastic language. It can accommodate quite onerous restrictions, unfortunately, on the President's power. But perhaps it can be read in a way that is not entirely unstructured and that heeds, if not the constitutional text that I mentioned, at least the objectives for setting up a unitary executive—namely, energy, faction control, and accountability. If you read it this way, if the restriction frustrates, or thwarts the President's ability to discharge any of those functions, then it would be seen as violating the *Morrison* test. That could lead to a fairly strong degree of presidential control over the work of the administrative agencies in the area of policy making.

In order to resist this argument, there should be some reason to believe that limiting presidential control, in a particular area, would not frustrate those objectives. Take, for example, the passage in *Morrison* where the Court seemed to signal that it would be permissible to restrict presidential control of quasi-judicial proceedings. It's easy to envision the argument under *Morrison* that presidential involvement in that area would not be needed to serve the objectives that I mentioned, because the model of litigation deals with all of those issues in other ways.

In the area of rulemaking, as I read the literature, there are three counter-arguments that have principally been raised. Argument one, that even though we now recognize that rulemaking has a very large policy making component, it still has an element of expertise that shouldn't be overridden by politics. Argument two is basically a due process argument. White House involvement may be unfair to other participants in the process. Argument three is that disclosing presidential or White House involvement promotes a kind of accountability by letting people know what went on.

I won't try to assess these arguments, but will say just in closing, that if the debate on the constitutionality of restrictions on presidential oversight is conducted in the terms that I've outlined, it will at least pay heed to the underlying considerations that led to the adoption of the unitary executive.

2

U.S. Supreme Court Says All Executive Power Is Not Vested in the President

Douglas T. Kendall

Douglas T. Kendall is Community Rights Counsel's [CRC] founder and executive director. He is coauthor of three CRC books, the lead author of numerous CRC reports and studies, and a contributor to publications such as the Virginia Law Review, *the* Harvard Environmental Law Review, *the* Washington Post, USA Today, *and the* Los Angeles Times.

The U.S. Supreme Court has repeatedly ruled against the theory that the Constitution vests all federal executive power in the president, or unitary executive, especially the concept that the president has sole authority to execute the law or to decide whether a subordinate official is faithfully executing the law. In decisions spanning two centuries, the Court has rejected the concept that the three branches of the federal government have airtight, completely independent powers. Congress, for example, has constitutional authority to pass laws necessary to execute its own powers, authority that should not be subject to presidential interference. Likewise, employees of independent agencies must be allowed to perform their jobs without fear of reprisal from the president: The president should not have the power to dismiss any government official at will, including independent counsel investigating the president, by claiming that the official is not executing the laws faithfully, or within constitutional bounds.

Douglas T. Kendall, Jennifer Bradley, and Marguerite McConihe, "The Constitution and the Environment: A Report on the Troubling Record of Samuel A. Alito," Washington, D.C., Community Rights Counsel, 2005.

In a 2000 speech to the Federalist Society, Judge Samuel A. Alito endorsed what he called "the theory of the unitary executive." Harkening back to his work as a Deputy Assistant Attorney General in the Office of Legal Counsel (OLC) of the Reagan Justice Department, Alito stated that "We [at OLC] were strong proponents of the theory of the unitary executive, that all federal executive power is vested by the Constitution in the President. And I thought then, and I still think, that this theory best captures the meaning of the Constitution's text and structure. . . ."

These were notable statements for a lower federal court judge to make, because, as Alito recognized later in his speech, the Supreme Court "had not exactly adopted the theory of the unitary executive." Rather, in *Morrison v. Olson*, the Court rejected this theory by a vote of 7–1. Thus, Alito was aligning himself with what he had previously described as Justice Antonin Scalia's "brilliant, but very lonely" dissent in *Morrison*, and against Chief Justice William Rehnquist's majority opinion. . . .

A Short History of the Theory of the Unitary Executive

It is a historical fact that our Constitution establishes a "unitary" executive. The Executive power is vested in the President, not, for example, a cabinet or a privy council. And Office of Legal Counsel (OLC) has an obligation "to assert and maintain the legitimate powers of privileges of the President against inadvertent or intentional congressional intrusion."

But when Judge Alito refers to the "theory of the unitary executive" he is referring to a particularly aggressive formulation of executive powers advocated during his years at OLC and rejected subsequently by both the Supreme Court and by Alito's successors at OLC. A report by the Congressional Research Service, published in 1987, the year Alito left OLC, chronicles the development of this theory. As this report's "abstract" explains: "In support of a variety of actions since 1981 designed to ensure ultimate presidential control of decision-making in all executive branch agencies, the Reagan administration has articulated a constitutional based theory of a unitary executive."

While this theory promotes expansive Presidential power, CRS explains, its development was "motivated by a limited-government, deregulatory ideology." The idea was to gain complete Presidential control over the functioning of the executive branch and then to use that control to shrink the size of the federal government. The administration proposed a "highly centralized bureaucratic structure of government" where the President possessed "broad supervisory and managerial powers as well as an encompassing political presence in administrative agencies."

Interpreting our framing document is the most important and awesome responsibility of a Supreme Court Justice.

This theory of a unitary executive is premised upon two general provisions of Article II of the Constitution, the "vesting clause" (Article II, § 1, clause 1), which provides that "The executive Power shall be vested in a President of the United States" and (2) the "take care" provision (Article II, § 3), giving the President the responsibility to "take Care that the Laws be faithfully executed." Proponents of this theory read these provisions together, and in conjunction with other constitutional provisions such as the Appointments Clause, to establish a general bar against Congressional interference with the President's discretion in executing the law.

Thus, for example, while Alito was at OLC he served as the lead counsel for the Department of Justice in what appears to be the first legal brief submitted by the Department arguing that portions of the independent counsel statute were unconstitutional because the independent counsel was not removable at will by the president or the attorney general. Alito's brief asserted that "subordinate executive offices created by statute possess no constitutional power independent of the President. Any executive power authorized by such offices is the President's power and therefore must be exercised in accordance with his direction." While recognizing that the Supreme Court had, for more than a century, permitted Congress to limit the President's ability to fire an "inferior" federal officer except for misconduct or other "cause," Alito opined that these precedents could be construed as permitting removal whenever "the president believed the inferior officer not to be executing the laws faithfully." The Supreme Court ultimately rejected precisely this argument in *Morrison v. Olson* and upheld the constitutionality of the independent counsel statute by a vote of 7–1.

The Theory of the Unitary Executive Critiqued

In his 2000 Federalist Society speech, Judge Alito asserted that the Constitution's text and structure support the Supreme Court's adoption of the theory of the unitary executive. This is a serious claim, because interpreting our framing document is the most important and awesome responsibility of a Supreme Court Justice. But, as explained by the Supreme Court throughout its 215-year history, his reading of the Constitution's text is neither the only, nor the best, reading of the Constitution's text and structure.

Indeed, Chief Justice William Rehnquist—who served as head of OLC under another strong proponent of executive power, President Richard Nixon—dismissed in a footnote what he called Justice Scalia's "rigid demarcation" of executive powers in *Morrison*:

> The dissent says that the language of Article II vesting the executive power of the United States in the President requires that every officer of the United States exercising any

part of that power must serve at the pleasure of the President and be removable by him at will. This rigid demarcation—a demarcation incapable of being altered by law in the slightest degree, and applicable to tens of thousands of holders of offices neither known nor foreseen by the Framers—depends upon an extrapolation from general constitutional language which we think is more than the text will bear. It is also contrary to our holding in *United States v. Perkins*, decided more than a century ago.

In fact, the Court has repeatedly rejected the "archaic view of the separation of powers as requiring three airtight departments of government." Instead, the Court has concluded that:

While the Constitution diffuses power the better to secure liberty, it also contemplates that practice will integrate the dispersed powers into a workable government. It enjoins upon its branches separateness but independence, autonomy but reciprocity.

Specifically, the Constitution couples the broad language of Article II (which is Alito's admitted focus), with equally broad language in Article I (which Alito seems to largely ignore) giving Congress a number of specific powers as well as the power to "make all laws which shall be necessary and proper for carrying into execution the foregoing Powers [of Congress], and all other Powers vested in this Constitution in the Government of the United States, or in any department or officer thereof." As Chief Justice John Marshall opined for the Supreme Court almost two centuries ago, the Constitution permits Congress "to exercise its best judgment in the selection of measures to carry into execution the Constitutional powers of the government."

The Constitution thus provides [according to the Court,] "a degree of overlapping responsibility, a duty of interdependence as well as independence." The reality of our Constitution's structure has translated into three general principles for resolving disputes between Congress and the President. First, the Court has been precise in following the Constitution's text where "[e]xplicit and unambiguous provisions of the Constitution prescribe and define just how powers are to be exercised." Second, the Court has fairly aggressively enforced an "anti-aggrandizement principle," striking down laws in which Congress takes executive power for itself.

This 'airtight' idea of separation of powers was rejected almost unanimously by the Court.

With respect to Congressional actions that are neither prescribed by a particular constitutional provision nor designed to aggrandize Congress's own power, however, the Court applies a more general test, asking if the legislation prevents the executive branch "from accomplishing its constitutionally assigned functions." Alito has criticized this effort to balance the authority of Congress to pass necessary and proper legislation with the President's executive authority as leading to results that depend at least in part on "the Court's subjective view at the time." But this describes much of constitutional law, and it is a product of the Framers' decision to provide the branches with "a degree of overlapping responsibility, a duty of interdependence as well as independence."

The "gospel according to OLC," practiced by Alito as an appointee in the Reagan Administration and preached by Alito after becoming a federal appellate judge, would replace this balancing test with a bright line rule that, when important executive functions are at issue, the president always wins. This might be a plausible reading of Article II were it written in isolation. But it is not, which is why this "airtight" idea of separation of powers was rejected almost unanimously by the Court in *Morrison* and why it no longer represents the position of OLC.

The Unitary Executive Theory in Supreme Court Case Law

Notwithstanding the Supreme Court's nearly unanimous rejection of the basic premise of the unitary executive theory in *Morrison*, Justice Scalia has remained a forceful proponent of this interpretation of the Constitution. Most importantly, as explained above, he has introduced the ideas and principles of the theory of the unitary executive into the debate over the constitutionality of environmental citizen suits and *qui tam* actions.

Another important example comes in *Printz v. United States*. In *Printz*, the Supreme Court ruled, 5 to 4, that sections of the Brady Handgun Violence Prevention Act were unconstitutional. The Act temporarily required local law enforcement officials to perform background checks on persons who purchased handguns from dealers until the U.S. Attorney General established a national system. Justice Scalia, writing for the majority, found this provision violated principles of constitutional federalism by "compel[ling] the States to enact or administer a federal regulatory program." The primary reasoning supporting the holding in *Printz* was the anti-commandeering principle that the Court had derived from the Constitution's Tenth Amendment in a prior case, *New York v. United States*.

Justice Scalia, however, offered a second justification for the holding: the Brady Act provisions violated separation of powers by "reducing the power of the Presidency." This short passage in *Printz* is the theory of the unitary executive, pure and simple. Justice Scalia asserts that the "Take Care" provision of Article II gives the power to enforce the laws solely to the President and those under his control; state officials under the Brady Act are not subject to "meaningful presidential control." Justice Scalia contends that the "unity in the Federal Executive . . . would be shattered" if Congress could act effectively without him simply by requiring state officers to execute its laws.

This passage was not necessary for the result in *Printz*, and it has not been employed by the Court in subsequent cases, but its potential significance has been noted by commentators across the political spectrum. Jay Bybee, now a judge on the Ninth Circuit and before that the head of OLC under President George W. Bush, claims that Justice Scalia "picked the Court's pocket clean on separation of powers" interjecting a "theory of the unitary executive that the remainder of the Court has never supported." Bybee argues that "Justice Scalia's separation of powers principle in *Printz* would ... threaten ... the independence of the fourth branch of government, the independent agencies." Laurence Tribe agrees:

> If this view of unitary and inviolable presidential power is actually embraced by a majority of the Court, then the constitutionality of much of the federal regulatory apparatus could be considered in grave doubt, for all genuinely independent agencies are of necessity directed by law officers over whom the President does not have unfettered removal power.

In dissent, Justice John Paul Stevens dismissed Scalia's unitary executive passage as "colorful hyperbole," but warned somewhat ominously that it "contradicts" prior holdings of the Court that approve a variety of cooperative federalism programs (including specifically the Clean Water Act and the Resource Conservation and Recovery Act), which employ state officials in the execution of federal laws.

3

The President's Signing Statements Are Legal and Useful

Douglas W. Kmiec

Douglas W. Kmiec is chair and professor of constitutional law at Pepperdine University in Malibu, California. Kmiec worked under President Ronald Reagan in the Justice Department's Office of Legal Counsel, which advises the executive branch on constitutional issues.

The president issues signing statements when signing a bill to comment on the provisions of the new law, set down directions for its implementation, and indicate that the new law will not be executed in a way that conflicts with the president's powers. The latter should not be interpreted as presidential defiance of the law. Rather, it is legal exercise of executive duty; the U.S. Constitution gives the president powers that prevail over Congress should a dispute arise over a law's execution. This executive power is not unchecked; the president is accountable to the electorate for the law's implementation. Signing statements are also valuable because of Congress's practice of adding controversial or unrelated riders to necessary, widely supported bills, taking advantage of the president's inability to veto only specific line items. A signing statement allows the president to sign important legislation but still alert Congress to provisions of the law he believes are constitutionally flawed or otherwise unacceptable in future legislation.

Douglas W. Kmiec, "It's Not Just Alito's Quandary: Reconciling Executive and Legislative Power," Findlaw.com, January 16, 2006. Reproduced by permission.

In his confirmation hearings, [as a Supreme Court justice] Judge Samuel Alito opined clearly and generally that no one, including the president, is above the law. Yet questioners also attempted to pull Alito into a current, more specific controversy: The rift between the President and Congress over the McCain Amendment limiting interrogation practice or the scope of executive power to undertake national security surveillance without specific court order pursuant to the Foreign Intelligence Surveillance Act (FISA).

Properly, Judge Alito refused to prejudge these questions— which could come before him as a Justice. Also properly, conceding the president to be Commander-in-Chief under the Constitution, Alito at the same time firmly acknowledged the limits of the Fourth Amendment and FISA.

Notwithstanding his well-considered, carefully-stated answers, Democratic members sought to portray Judge Alito as biased in favor of executive power, complaining of his belief in a unitary executive and his endorsement of presidential signing statements. Yet, as I will detail below, neither of these stances is at all "out of the mainstream," as Senator Charles E. Schumer likes to say—after all, the 1787 Constitutional Convention decisively rejected the concept of a plural executive.

Similarly, it should hardly be shocking—though Democrats seem to think so—that when President Bush signed the recent McCain legislation clarifying limits on wartime interrogations, he stated that the new law would not be construed in a manner contrary to the president's powers. There is no reason to believe that Bush was claiming he would not follow the law rather than merely re-stating a necessary principle of all statutory law—namely, that it must be consistent with the Constitution.

When the President and Congress Disagree on Interpretation

What happens, though, when the President's interpretation of a law differs from Congress' reading of what is constitutionally permissible?

In some ways, this is simply part of the ongoing dynamic of the separation of powers. The Framers expected that ambition would check ambition without the public being misled into thinking that we are facing a constitutional crisis. Congress and the President have the responsibility not to overreach, but if a trespass does occur, to address it without hyperbole or rushing into court.

If the president does have power derived from the Constitution, then the Supremacy Clause . . . ensures that the Constitution trumps statutes.

Premature litigation has risks on both sides: for the president, it risks exposure of classified materials as well as a possible adverse ruling. Recall the Supreme Court's *Youngstown* decision, reprimanding Harry Truman for seizing the steel mills. A decision from the High Court not only permanently constrains presidential power on the particular issue before the Court, but also, by its formal, binding language, might unwisely constrain executive authority as to other unforeseen issues.

And Congress is not assured judicial victory. It is not inconceivable that the Court might reaffirm equally venerable precedent like Curtiss-Wright or the Prize Cases that the president has foreign affairs authority that is inherent in sovereignty and not fully dependent upon constitutional language. Admittedly, FISA's own statutory wartime exception (excusing the warrant requirement for a brief period following a war declaration) is in tension with a sweeping inherent power claim. However, without knowing the exact contours of the external threat or the reasoning for not relying upon FISA, the president's claim simply cannot be assessed.

The bottom line: There is not a scholar alive who could confidently say who would prevail in a clash between a federal statute and the President's assertion of inherent power vis-à-vis the McCain Amendment, or, for that matter, war-on-terror-related wiretapping.

The Possibility of Nonjusticiability

Judge Alito and Senator Feingold tossed this dilemma back and forth during some of the hearings' more intelligible moments. Feingold seemed to want the judge to state categorically that in a clash between Congress and the President over a statute (such as McCain or FISA), the statute would prevail. But if the president does have power derived from the Constitution, then the Supremacy Clause—which ensures that the Constitution trumps statutes—obviously precludes the kind of simple answer Feingold was trying to elicit.

Judge Alito knew this. Thus, lacking the specific facts of an actual case, briefing, argument, and deliberation, he properly gave only an outline of what he described as a "momentous constitutional issue"—one that the Court might even find to be a nonjusticiable political question. (A legal question is "nonjusticiable" when it is held to be not susceptible to court resolution. When the Supreme Court finds a dispute nonjusticiable, it lacks jurisdiction, and can reach no result, one way or the other.)

The much maligned presidential signing statement is one ... avenue for dialogue. Rather than a veto—which ends debate—the signing statement extends the legislative conversation.

When the Constitution supplies no manageable standard by which to give resolution to a particular question, and foreign affairs is often such an area, the Court historically has left the elected branches to their own devices. Hearing the Court might opt not to intervene seemed to startle Senator Feingold, but it was a healthy reminder that political actors ought not, in a democracy, complacently expect either ready approbation or rescue from judges (or even from a Supreme Court nominee under pressure).

Signing Statements as a Means of Fostering Interbranch Dialogue

So what devices exist by which the political branches can continue their dialogue—rather than rushing into the federal courts, a move that has significant risks for all?

Ironically, the much-maligned presidential signing statement is one such avenue for dialogue. Rather than a veto—which ends debate, except in the unlikely event that a supermajority of Congress overrides it—the signing statement extends the legislative conversation. It sets forth the President's view—to which Congress then can respond.

The McCain law signing statement, for example, allowed the president to express overtly his reservation, while also allowing the legislative limitation on interrogation practice to, in the main, go into effect. This was hardly an insidious executive power play as some of the questioning posed to Judge Alito implied. Indeed, suggesting as much overlooks the utility, long history, and larger purposes of presidential signing statements.

Not a Power Grab

The use of presidential signing statements can be traced back at least to 1830, when President Andrew Jackson employed the device to give his interpretation of a road appropriation. When Sam Alito and I served together as constitutional legal counsel to Ronald Reagan, the President likewise employed this tradition to improve his overall supervision of the executive branch.

While Congress is the principal lawmaking body, laws do not implement themselves, and much law employs, as a result of compromise, imprecise language. Vague terms create room for interpretation and discretion, and thus, the question becomes: Who will exercise that discretion?

President Reagan felt the initial executive effort to interpret a law was his, since he would be the one held electorally accountable for that law's implementation. Were the President not to give direction as to the law's implementation, Reagan reasoned, the task would fall to a far less accountable and visible federal bureaucrat. In short, Reagan's purpose had nothing to do with wanting to substitute his judgment for that of Congress and the judiciary. His goal was to promote visibility and accountability in areas where interpretation is unavoidable—virtues that conservatives and liberals alike agree are central to our democracy.

As an aside, signing statements have special modern importance as Congress continues the practice of lumping together numerous unrelated provisions in omnibus bills—often inserting the most controversial provisions in emergency appropriations measures passed at, or after, fiscal deadlines. This practice effectively curtails the President's constitutionally provided veto authority. It also denies the people what Alexander Hamilton referred to as "the chances in favor of the community against the passing of bad laws, through haste, inadvertence, or design."

A Key Example

Practically, the president does not always have discretion *not* to sign legislation containing a constitutional defect. Consider, for example, Franklin Roosevelt's approval of the Lend-Lease Act, which provided vital support to our allies in World War II. Signing the act was necessary. Thus, pointing out its constitutionally problematic aspect was the President's best and only option.

As presented to the President, the Lend-Lease Act contained a provision for its termination by an unconstitutional means. Roosevelt correctly objected to this infringement of the presidential office.

Interestingly, then-Attorney General Robert Jackson, later a justice of the Supreme Court, was more equivocal about the constitutional problem than FDR, but Roosevelt would have none of it. In a rare twist, FDR issued a signing statement that was effectively a legal opinion to his own Attorney General, stating that he "felt constrained to sign the measure [to meet a momentous emergency of great magnitude in world affairs], in spite of the fact that it contained a provision which, in [his] opinion, is clearly unconstitutional."

Roosevelt then directed the Attorney General to put his commentary in the "official files of the Department of Justice" in order to preclude his approval of the Act from being used "as a precedent for any future legislation comprising provisions of a similar nature."

The signing statement reservation ought better be understood as an effort to alert, not scuttle, Congress.

Signing Statements Today

As dramatic as the Lend-Lease case is, it did not pose as great a problem as it might have, because there was little chance that the Congress was going to implement a questionable limitation in the midst of a World War. Then, it was clear that the political branches ought at least to strive to be of one mind vis-à-vis America's military antagonists, and to send one message.

It can hardly be said that a similar comity exists between the President and Congress in today's war on terror. Though both agree that since 9/11, America has faced grave, imminent harm, highly significant differences in approach remain and need better resolution.

President Bush's signing statement, then, ought to be viewed as an occasion for the political branches to reason this through, rather than engaging in all-or-nothing accusations of bad faith. Possibly, some compromise can be reached. In light of reported torture abuses, the McCain Amendment's limitations on "cruel, inhuman, and degrading treatment" seem generally apt, and with respect to eavesdropping, the FISA structure appears generally sound. But if there are specific needs that justify exceptional practices under either law to secure the nation's safety, the president is right to see them as part of his constitutional duty, and the signing statement reservation ought better be understood as an effort to alert, not scuttle, Congress. The president and Congress have a common enemy, after all, and it is not themselves. . . .

Chief Justice John Marshall started the American judicial enterprise in the famous case of *Marbury v. Madison* by observing that "an act of the legislature, repugnant to the Constitution, is void." His fellow justice, James Wilson, a principal drafter of the Constitution, likewise wrote that "the President of the United States could . . . refuse to carry into effect an act that violates the Constitution."

Substantively, I suspect Senator Feingold might disagree. But certainly the clarity of these founding expressions is remarkable. But then, neither Marshall nor Wilson is seeking confirmation today.

4

The President's Signing Statements Are an Abuse of Executive Power

John Dean

John Dean, former White House counsel to President Richard M. Nixon during the Watergate investigation involving abuses of executive authority, is a writer, columnist, and lecturer on law, government, and politics.

Several presidents have used signing statements to indicate their displeasure with provisions of laws passed by Congress that they do not wish to veto. However, President George W. Bush has taken signing statements to an extreme level; he has used signing statements to raise more than five hundred challenges to various provisions but has yet to veto a single bill. Bush's use of signing statements is an ambitious attempt to bolster presidential powers without giving Congress a chance to override a veto; his statements often flatly reject the law or maintain that mandatory provisions are merely "advisory." In effect, he is using signing statements as a line-item veto, which the Supreme Court has ruled is unconstitutional. If a president believes a law's provision is unconstitutional, he must veto the entire bill and not attempt to nullify only a portion of it with a signing statement.

Presidential signing statements are old news to anyone who has served in the White House counsel's office. Presidents have long used them to add their two cents when a law passed

John Dean, "The Problem with Presidential Signing Statements: Their Use and Misuse by the Bush Administration," FindLaw.com, January 13, 2006. Reproduced by permission.

by Congress has provisions they do not like, yet they are not inclined to veto it. Nixon's statements, for example, often related to spending authorization laws which he felt were excessive and contrary to his fiscal policies.

In this column, I'll take a close look at President George W. Bush's use of signing statements. I find these signing statements are to Bush and Dick Cheney's presidency what steroids were to Arnold Schwarzenegger's body building. Like Schwarzenegger with his steroids, Bush does not deny using his signing statements; does not like talking about using them; and believes that they add muscle.

But like steroids, signing statements ultimately lead to serious trouble.

Relying on Command, Rather than Persuasion

Phillip Cooper is a leading expert on signing statements. His 2002 book, *By Order of the President: The Use and Abuse of Executive Direct Action*, assesses the uses and abuses of signing statements by presidents Ronald Reagan, George H.W. Bush and Bill Clinton. Cooper has updated his material in a recent essay for the *Presidential Studies Quarterly*, to encompass the use of signing statements by now-President Bush as well.

Bush is using his signing statements to effectively nullify [laws] as they relate to the executive branch.

By Cooper's count, George W. Bush issued 23 signing statements in 2001; 34 statements in 2002, raising 168 constitutional objections; 27 statements in 2003, raising 142 constitutional challenges, and 23 statements in 2004, raising 175 constitutional criticisms. In total, during his first term Bush raised a remarkable 505 constitutional challenges to various provisions of legislation that became law.

That number may be approaching 600 challenges by now. Yet Bush has not vetoed a single bill, notwithstanding all these claims, in his own signing statements, that they are unconstitutional insofar as they relate to him.

Rather than veto laws passed by Congress, Bush is using his signing statements to effectively nullify them as they relate to the executive branch. These statements, for him, function as directives to executive branch departments and agencies as to how they are to implement the relevant law.

President Bush and the attorneys advising him may also anticipate that the signing statements will help him if and when the relevant laws are construed in court—for federal courts, depending on their views of executive power, may deem such statements relevant to their interpretation of a given law. After all, the law would not have passed had the President decided to veto it, so arguably, his view on what the law meant ought to (within reason) carry some weight for the court interpreting it. This is the argument, anyway.

Bush has quietly been using these statements to bolster presidential powers. It is a calculated, systematic scheme that has gone largely unnoticed (even though these statements are published in the *Weekly Compilation of Presidential Documents*) until recently, when President Bush used a signing statement to attempt to nullify the recent, controversial McCain amendment regarding torture, which drew some media attention.

Pumping Up the Bush Presidency with Signing Statements

Generally, Bush's signing statements tend to be brief and very broad, and they seldom cite the authority on which the president is relying for his reading of the law. None has yet been tested in court. But they do appear to be bulking up the powers of the presidency. Here are a few examples:

Suppose a new law requires the President to act in a certain manner—for instance, to report to Congress on how he is dealing with terrorism. Bush's signing statement will flat out reject the law, and state that he will construe the law "in a manner consistent with the President's constitutional authority to withhold information the disclosure of which could impair foreign relations, the national security, the deliberative processes of the Executive, or the performance of the Executive's constitutional duties."

The upshot? It is as if no law had been passed on the matter at all.

The President's signing statements are, in some instances, effectively rewriting the laws by reinterpreting how the law will be implemented.

Or suppose a new law suggests even the slightest intrusion into the President's undefined "prerogative powers" under Article II of the Constitution, relating to national security, intelligence gathering, or law enforcement. Bush's signing statement will claim that notwithstanding the clear intent of Congress, which has used mandatory language, the provision will be considered as "advisory."

The upshot? It is as if Congress had acted as a mere advisor, with no more formal power than, say, [Bush's senior adviser] Karl Rove—not as a coordinate and coequal branch of government, which in fact it is.

As Phillip Cooper observes, the President's signing statements are, in some instances, effectively rewriting the laws by reinterpreting how the law will be implemented. Notably, Cooper finds some of Bush's signing statements—and he has the benefit of judging them against his extensive knowledge of other Presidents' signing statements—"excessive, unhelpful, and needlessly confrontational."

The Problems with Bush's Use of Signing Statements

Given the incredible number of constitutional challenges Bush is issuing to new laws, without vetoing them, his use of signing statements is going to sooner or later put him in an untenable position. And there is a strong argument that it has already put him in a position contrary to Supreme Court precedent, and the Constitution, vis-à-vis the veto power.

Bush is using signing statements like line item vetoes. Yet the Supreme Court has held the line item vetoes are unconstitutional. In 1988, in *Clinton v. New York*, the High Court said a president had to veto an entire law: Even Congress, with its Line Item Veto Act, could not permit him to veto provisions he might not like.

The Court held the Line Item Veto Act unconstitutional in that it violated the Constitution's Presentment Clause. That Clause says that after a bill has passed both Houses, but "before it become[s] a Law," it must be presented to the President, who "shall sign it" if he approves it, but "return it" —that is, veto the bill, in its entirety—if he does not.

Signing statements often ignore the fact that only Congress can create all the departments and agencies of the Executive Branch, and only Congress can fund these operations.

Following the Court's logic, and the spirit of the Presentment Clause, a president who finds part of a bill unconstitutional, ought to veto the entire bill—not sign it with reservations in a way that attempts to effectively veto part (and only part) of the bill. Yet that is exactly what Bush is doing. The Presentment Clause makes clear that the veto power is to be used with respect to a bill in its entirety, not in part.

The frequency and the audacity of Bush's use of signing statements are troubling. Enactments by Congress are presumed to be constitutional—as the Justice Department has often reiterated. For example, take what is close to boilerplate language from a government brief (selected at random): "It is well-established that Congressional legislation is entitled to a strong presumption of constitutionality. See *United States v. Morrison*. ('Every possible presumption is in favor of the validity of a statute, and this continues until the contrary is shown beyond a rational doubt.')"

Bush's use of signing statements thus potentially brings him into conflict with his own Justice Department. The Justice Department is responsible for defending the constitutionality of laws enacted by Congress. What is going to happen when the question at issue is the constitutionality of a provision the President has declared unconstitutional in a signing statement?

Does the President's signing statement overcome the presumption of constitutionality? I doubt it. Will the Department of Justice have a serious conflict of interest? For certain, it will.

It is remarkable that Bush believes he can ignore a law, and protect himself, through a signing statement.

Should thus Congress establish its own non-partisan legal division, not unlike the Congressional Reference Service, to protect its interests, since the Department of Justice may have conflicts? It's something to think about.

These are just a few practical and constitutional problems that arise when a president acts as if there is his government, and then there is the Congress' government. Signing statements often ignore the fact that only Congress can create all the departments and agencies of the Executive Branch, and only Congress can fund these operations.

And the power to create and fund is also, by implication, the power to regulate and to oversee. Congress can, to some extent, direct how these agencies will function without infringing on presidential power.

Impact of Presidential Signing Statements

The immediate impact of signing statements, of course, is felt within the Executive Branch: As I noted, Bush's statements will likely have a direct influence on how that branch's agencies and departments interpret and enforce the law.

It is remarkable that Bush believes he can ignore a law, and protect himself, through a signing statement. Despite the McCain Amendment's clear anti-torture stance, the military may feel free to use torture anyway, based on the President's attempt to use a signing statement to wholly undercut the bill.

This kind of expansive use of a signing statement presents not only Presentment Clause problems, but also clashes with the Constitutional implication that a veto is the President's only and exclusive avenue to prevent a bill's becoming law. The powers of foot-dragging and resistance-by-signing-statement, are not mentioned in the Constitution alongside the veto, after all. Congress wanted to impeach Nixon for impounding money he thought should not be spent. Telling Congress its laws do not apply makes Nixon's impounding look like cooperation with Congress, by comparison.

The longer term impact of signing statements is potentially grave—and is being ignored by the Bush administration. But it cannot be ignored forever. Defiance by Bush of Congressional lawmaking will come back to haunt this President.

Watergate was about abuse of power. Nixon, not unlike Bush, insisted on pushing the powers of the presidency to, and beyond, their limits. But as Nixon headed into his second term with even grander plans than he'd had in the first term, the Congress became concerned. (And for good reason.)

Bush, who has been pushing the envelope on presidential powers, is just beginning to learn what kind of Congressional blowback can result.

First, there are the leaks: People within the Executive branch become troubled by a president's overreaching. When Nixon adopted extreme measures, people within the administration began leaking. The same is now happening to Bush, for there was the leak about the use of torture. And, more recently, there was the leak as to the use of warrantless electronic surveillance on Americans.

Once the leaks start, they continue, and Congressional ire is not far behind. The overwhelming Congressional support for Senator John McCain's torture ban suggests, too, that Congress will not be happy if leaks begin to suggest the President—as his signing statement foreshadows—is already flouting the ban.

In short, Bush's signing statements, which are now going over the top, are going to cause a Congressional reaction. It is inevitable. If Republicans lose control of either the House or Senate—and perhaps even if they don't, if the subject is torture or an egregious violation of civil liberties—then the Bush/ Cheney administration will wish it had not issued all those signing statements.

Indeed, the Administration may be eating its words—with Congress holding the plate out, and forcing the unconstitutional verbiage back down. That, in the end, is the only kind of torture Americans ought to countenance.

5

The President's Terrorist Surveillance Program Is Lawful and Necessary

Alberto Gonzales

Alberto Gonzales is attorney general under President George W. Bush, whom he previously served as White House counsel from 2001–2005. Gonzalez is a former Texas Supreme Court justice and Texas secretary of state.

The president's primary responsibility under the U.S. Constitution is to protect America's national security. During time of war, as commander in chief the president has ultimate authority to order military operations, which traditionally includes surveillance of the nation's enemies and suspected enemies without a warrant. The surveillance program used against al-Qaeda as part of the war on terrorism has been examined by the Department of Justice, the attorney general, and other government lawyers, all of whom have determined that it is lawful. Furthermore, a congressional resolution has authorized the president to use "all necessary and appropriate force" against America's enemies. The president's terrorist surveillance program is therefore necessary and lawful to prevent terrorist attack.

Just after dawn on September 11th, 2001, I flew out of Dulles Airport less than an hour before the departure from the same airport of American Airlines Flight 77, the plane that was hijacked and crashed into the Pentagon later that morn-

Alberto Gonzales, "Prepared Remarks for Attorney General Alberto R. Gonzales at the Georgetown University Law Center," January 24, 2006.

ing. When I arrived in Norfolk, Virginia, to give a speech, the North Tower of the World Trade Center had been hit. By the end of my remarks, both the North and South Towers stood shrouded in smoke and flames with many desperate people jumping to their deaths, some 90 stories below. I spent much of the rest of that horrible day trying to get back to Washington to assist the President in my role as White House Counsel.

Everyone has a story from that morning. Up and down the East Coast, men and women were settling into their desks, coming home from a graveyard shift, or taking their children to school. And across the rest of the country, Americans were waking up to smoldering ruins and the images of ash covered faces. We remember where we were, what we were doing ... and how we felt on that terrible morning, as 3,000 innocent men, women, and children died, without warning, without being able to look into the faces of their loved ones and say goodbye ... all killed just for being Americans.

The open wounds so many of us carry from that day are the backdrop to the current debate about the National Security Agency's terrorist surveillance program. This program, described by the President, is focused on international communications where experienced intelligence experts have reason to believe that at least one party to the communication is a member or agent of al Qaeda or a terrorist organization affiliated with al Qaeda. This program is reviewed and reauthorized by the President approximately every 45 days. The leadership of Congress, including the leaders of the Intelligence Committees of both Houses of Congress, have been briefed about this program more than a dozen times since 2001....

Whatever your opinion, this much is clear: No one is above the law. We are all bound by the Constitution, and no matter the pain and anger we feel from the attacks, we must all abide by the Constitution. ... The President takes seriously his obligations to protect the American people and to protect the Constitution, and he is committed to upholding both of those obligations.

I've noticed that through all of the noise on this topic, very few have asked that the terrorist surveillance program be stopped. The American people are, however, asking two important questions: Is this program necessary? And is it lawful? The answer to each is yes.

A Nation at War

The question of necessity rightly falls to our nation's military leaders. You've heard the President declare: We are a nation at war. . . .

The conflict against al Qaeda is, in fundamental respects, a war of information. We cannot build walls thick enough, fences high enough, or systems strong enough to keep our enemies out of our open and welcoming country. Instead, as the bipartisan 9/11 and WMD [Weapons of Mass Destruction] Commissions have urged, we must understand better who they are and what they're doing—we have to collect more dots, if you will, before we can "connect the dots." This program to surveil al Qaeda is a necessary weapon as we fight to detect and prevent another attack before it happens. I feel confident that is what the American people expect . . . and it's what the terrorist surveillance program provides. . . .

The Justice Department thoroughly examined this program against al Qaeda, and concluded that the President is acting within his power in authorizing it.

The Surveillance Is Lawful

Now, the legal authorities. As Attorney General, I am primarily concerned with the legal basis for these necessary military activities. I expect that as lawyers and law students, you are too.

The Attorney General of the United States is the chief legal advisor for the Executive Branch. Accordingly, from the outset, the Justice Department thoroughly examined this program against al Qaeda, and concluded that the President is acting within his power in authorizing it. These activities are lawful. The Justice Department is not alone in reaching that conclusion. Career lawyers at the NSA and the NSA's Inspector General have been intimately involved in reviewing the program and ensuring its legality.

The terrorist surveillance program is firmly grounded in the President's constitutional authorities. No other public official—no mayor, no governor, no member of Congress—is charged by the Constitution with the primary responsibility for protecting the safety of all Americans—and the Constitution gives the President all authority necessary to fulfill this solemn duty.

It has long been recognized that the President's constitutional powers include the authority to conduct warrantless surveillance aimed at detecting and preventing armed attacks on the United States. Presidents have uniformly relied on their inherent power to gather foreign intelligence for reasons both diplomatic and military, and the federal courts have consistently upheld this long-standing practice.

If this is the case in ordinary times, it is even more so in the present circumstances of our armed conflict with al Qaeda and its allies. The terrorist surveillance program was authorized in response to the deadliest foreign attack on American soil, and it is designed solely to prevent the next attack. After all, the goal of our enemy is to blend in with our civilian population in order to plan and carry out future attacks within America. We cannot forget that the 9/11 hijackers were in our country, living in our communities.

The President's authority to take military action—including the use of communications intelligence targeted at the enemy—does not come merely from his inherent constitutional powers. It comes directly from Congress as well.

The Authorization for Use of Military Force

Just a few days after the events of September 11th, Congress enacted a joint resolution to support and authorize a military response to the attacks on American soil. In this resolution, the Authorization for Use of Military Force, Congress did two important things. First, it expressly recognized the President's "authority under the Constitution to take action to deter and prevent acts of international terrorism against the United States." Second, it supplemented that authority by authorizing the President to, quote, "use all necessary and appropriate force against those nations, organizations, or persons he determines planned, authorized, committed, or aided the terrorist attacks" in order to prevent further attacks on the United States.

As long as electronic communications have existed, the United States has conducted surveillance of those communications during wartime—all without judicial warrant.

The Resolution means that the President's authority to use military force against those terrorist groups is at its maximum because he is acting with the express authorization of Congress. Thus, were we to employ the three-part framework of Justice [Robert H.] Jackson's concurring opinion in the Youngstown Steel Seizure case, the President's authority falls within Category One, and is at its highest. He is acting "pursuant to an express or implied authorization of Congress," and the President's authority "includes all that he possesses in his own right [under the Constitution] plus all that Congress can" confer on him.

In 2004, the Supreme Court considered the scope of the Force Resolution in the *Hamdi* case. There, the question was whether the President had the authority to detain an American citizen as an enemy combatant for the duration of the hostilities.

In that case, the Supreme Court confirmed that the expansive language of the Resolution—"all necessary and appropriate force"—ensures that the congressional authorization extends to traditional incidents of waging war. And, just like the detention of enemy combatants approved in *Hamdi*, the use of communications intelligence to prevent enemy attacks is a fundamental and well-accepted incident of military force.

A Tradition of Wartime Enemy Surveillance

This fact is borne out by history. This Nation has a long tradition of wartime enemy surveillance—a tradition that can be traced to George Washington, who made frequent and effective use of secret intelligence, including the interception of mail between the British and Americans.

And for as long as electronic communications have existed, the United States has conducted surveillance of those communications during wartime—all without judicial warrant. In the Civil War, for example, telegraph wiretapping was common, and provided important intelligence for both sides. In World War I, President Wilson ordered the interception of all cable communications between the United States and Europe; he inferred the authority to do so from the Constitution and from a general congressional authorization to use military force that did not mention anything about such surveillance. So too in World War II; the day after the attack on Pearl Harbor, President Roosevelt authorized the interception of all communications traffic into and out of the United States. The terrorist surveillance program, of course, is far more focused, since it involves only the interception of international communications that are linked to al Qaeda or its allies.

Some have suggested that the Force Resolution did not authorize intelligence collection inside the United States. That contention cannot be squared with the reality of the 9/11 attacks, which gave rise to the Resolution, and with the language of the authorization itself, which calls on the President to protect Americans both "at home and abroad" and to take action to prevent further terrorist attacks "against the United States." It's also contrary to the history of wartime surveillance, which has often involved the interception of enemy communications into and out of the United States.

Against this backdrop, the NSA's focused terrorist surveillance program falls squarely within the broad authorization of the Resolution even though, as some have argued, the Resolution does not expressly mention surveillance. The Resolution also doesn't mention detention of enemy combatants. But we know from the Supreme Court's decision in *Hamdi* that such detention is authorized. Justice Sandra Day O'Connor reasoned: "Because detention to prevent a combatant's return to the battlefield is a fundamental incident of waging war . . . Congress has clearly and unmistakably authorized detention in the narrow circumstances considered here."

As Justice O'Connor recognized, it does not matter that the Force Resolution nowhere specifically refers to the detention of U.S. citizens as enemy combatants. Nor does it matter that individual Members of Congress may not have specifically intended to authorize such detention. The same is true of electronic surveillance. It is a traditional incident of war and, thus, as Justice O'Connor said, it is "of no moment" that the Resolution does not explicitly mention this activity.

These omissions are not at all surprising. In enacting the Force Resolution, Congress made no attempt to catalog every aspect of the use of force it was authorizing.

Instead, following the model of past military force authorizations, Congress—in general, but broad, terms—confirmed the President's authority to use all traditional and legitimate incidents of military force to identify and defeat the enemy. In doing so, Congress must be understood to have intended that the use of electronic surveillance against the enemy is a fundamental component of military operations.

The Force Resolution provides the relevant statutory authorization for the terrorist surveillance program.

The Foreign Intelligence Surveillance Act

Some contend that even if the President has constitutional authority to engage in the surveillance of our enemy in a time of war, that authority has been constrained by Congress with the passage in 1978 of the Foreign Intelligence Surveillance Act. Generally, FISA requires the government to obtain an order from a special FISA court before conducting electronic surveillance. . . .

First, FISA, of course, allows Congress to respond to new threats through separate legislation. FISA bars persons from intentionally "engag[ing] . . . in electronic surveillance under color of law except as authorized by statute." For the reasons I have already discussed, the Force Resolution provides the relevant statutory authorization for the terrorist surveillance program. *Hamdi* makes it clear that the broad language in the Resolution can satisfy a requirement for specific statutory authorization set forth in another law.

Hamdi involved a statutory prohibition on all detention of U.S. citizens except as authorized "pursuant to an Act of Congress." Even though the detention of a U.S. citizen involves a deprivation of liberty, and even though the Force Resolution says nothing on its face about detention of U.S. citizens, a majority of the members of the Court nevertheless concluded that the Resolution satisfied the statutory requirement. The same is true, I submit, for the prohibition on warrantless electronic surveillance in FISA.

You may have heard about the provision of FISA that allows the President to conduct warrantless surveillance for 15 days following a declaration of war. That provision shows that Congress knew that warrantless surveillance would be essential in wartime. But no one could reasonably suggest that all such critical military surveillance in a time of war would end after only 15 days.

Instead, the legislative history of this provision makes it clear that Congress elected NOT TO DECIDE how surveillance might need to be conducted in the event of a particular armed conflict. Congress expected that it would revisit the issue in light of events and likely would enact a special authorization during that 15-day period. That is exactly what happened three days after the attacks of 9/11, when Congress passed the Force Resolution, permitting the President to exercise "all necessary and appropriate" incidents of military force.

Thus, it is simply not the case that Congress in 1978 anticipated all the ways that the President might need to act in times of armed conflict to protect the United States. FISA, by its own terms, was not intended to be the last word on these critical issues.

It is imperative for national security that we can detect RELIABLY, IMMEDIATELY, and WITHOUT DELAY whenever communications associated with al Qaeda enter or leave the United States.

"Except as Authorized by Statute"

Second, some people have argued that, by their terms, Title III and FISA are the "exclusive means" for conducting electronic surveillance. It is true that the law says that Title III and FISA are "the exclusive means by which electronic surveillance . . . may be conducted." But, as I have said before, FISA itself says elsewhere that the government cannot engage in electronic surveillance "except as authorized by statute." It is noteworthy that, FISA did not say "the government cannot engage in electronic surveillance 'except as authorized by FISA and Title III.'" No, it said, except as authorized by statute—any statute. And, in this case, that other statute is the Force Resolution.

Even if some might think that's not the only way to read the statute, in accordance with long recognized canons of construction, FISA must be interpreted in harmony with the Force Resolution to allow the President, as Commander-in-Chief during time of armed conflict, to take the actions necessary to protect the country from another catastrophic attack. So long as such an interpretation is "fairly possible," the Supreme Court has made clear that it must be adopted, in order to avoid the serious constitutional issues that would otherwise be raised.

Reliably, Immediately, and Without Delay

Third, I keep hearing, "Why not FISA?" "Why didn't the President get orders from the FISA court approving these NSA intercepts of al Qaeda communications?"

We have to remember that we're talking about a wartime foreign intelligence program. It is an "early warning system" with only one purpose: To detect and prevent the next attack on the United States from foreign agents hiding in our midst. It is imperative for national security that we can detect RELIABLY, IMMEDIATELY, and WITHOUT DELAY whenever communications associated with al Qaeda enter or leave the United States. That may be the only way to alert us to the presence of an al Qaeda agent in our country and to the existence of an unfolding plot.

Consistent with the wartime intelligence nature of this program, the optimal way to achieve the necessary speed and agility is to leave the decisions about particular intercepts to the judgment of professional intelligence officers, based on the best available intelligence information. They can make that call quickly. If, however, those same intelligence officers had to navigate through the FISA process for each of these intercepts, that would necessarily introduce a significant factor of DE-LAY, and there would be critical holes in our early warning system.

Some have pointed to the provision in FISA that allows for so-called "emergency authorizations" of surveillance for 72 hours without a court order. There's a serious misconception about these emergency authorizations. People should know that we do not approve emergency authorizations without knowing that we will receive court approval within 72 hours. FISA requires the Attorney General to determine IN AD-VANCE that a FISA application for that particular intercept will be fully supported and will be approved by the court before an emergency authorization may be granted. That review process can take precious time.

Thus, to initiate surveillance under a FISA emergency authorization, it is not enough to rely on the best judgment of our intelligence officers alone. Those intelligence officers would have to get the sign-off of lawyers at the NSA that all provisions of FISA have been satisfied, then lawyers in the Department of Justice would have to be similarly satisfied, and finally as Attorney General, I would have to be satisfied that the search meets the requirements of FISA. And we would have to be prepared to follow up with a full FISA application within the 72 hours.

A typical FISA application involves a substantial process in its own right: The work of several lawyers; the preparation of a legal brief and supporting declarations; the approval of a Cabinet-level officer; a certification from the National Security Adviser, the Director of the FBI, or another designated Senate-confirmed officer; and, finally, of course, the approval of an Article III judge.

We all agree that there should be appropriate checks and balances on our branches of government. The FISA process makes perfect sense in almost all cases of foreign intelligence monitoring in the United States. Although technology has changed dramatically since FISA was enacted, FISA remains a vital tool in the War on Terror, and one that we are using to its fullest and will continue to use against al Qaeda and other foreign threats. But as the President has explained, the terrorist surveillance program operated by the NSA requires the maximum in speed and agility, since even a very short delay may make the difference between success and failure in preventing the next attack. And we cannot afford to fail. . . .

It is hard to imagine a President who wouldn't elect to use these tools in defense of the American people—in fact, I think it would be irresponsible to do otherwise.

I close with a reminder that [in January 2006], al Jazeera aired an audio tape in which Osama bin Laden promised a new round of attacks on the United States. Bin Laden said the proof of his promise is, and I quote, "the explosions you have seen in the capitals of European nations." He continued, quote, "The delay in similar operations happening in America has not been because of failure to break through your security measures. The operations are under preparation and you will see them in your homes the minute they are through with preparations." Close quote.

We've seen and heard these types of warnings before. And we've seen what the result of those preparations can be— thousands of our fellow citizens who perished in the attacks of 9/11.

This Administration has chosen to act now to prevent the next attack, rather than wait until it is too late. This Administration has chosen to utilize every necessary and lawful tool at its disposal. It is hard to imagine a President who wouldn't elect to use these tools in defense of the American people—in fact, I think it would be irresponsible to do otherwise.

Shelved with Opposing Viewpoints

Firefighter from Laney Children's Center

The Laney Library celebrated Halloween this year with a visit from the Laney Children's Center and Jack-o'-lantern Decoration Contest. More pictures posted on the library website:

The terrorist surveillance program is both necessary and lawful. Accordingly, the President has done with this lawful authority the only responsible thing: use it. He has exercised, and will continue to exercise, his authority to protect Americans and the cherished freedoms of the American people.

6

The President's Terrorist Surveillance Program Is Illegal

American Civil Liberties Union

The American Civil Liberties Union, founded in 1920, is a national nonprofit, nonpartisan organization that works to defend Americans' civil rights as guaranteed in the U.S. Constitution.

In 2002 President George W. Bush issued an order allowing the National Security Agency to monitor international and domestic phone calls and e-mails of U.S. citizens and legal residents without judicial warrant. First publicly reported in December 2005, this order is illegal and an abuse of executive power. The Fourth Amendment to the U.S. Constitution and surveillance laws passed by Congress require judicial oversight of all government eavesdropping. There are only three laws that permit the government to spy on its citizens, residents, and agents of foreign powers, and neither Bush nor his agents followed the requirements of any of these laws. The president's claim that he can bypass the Constitution and surveillance laws because he is the commander in chief is an attempt at an end-run around the courts. Even the president of the United States is bound by the rule of law.

W hat if it emerged that the President of the United States was flagrantly violating the Constitution and a law passed by the Congress to protect Americans against abuses by a super-secret spy agency? What if, instead of apologizing, he said, in essence, "I have the power to do that, because I say I can." That frightening scenario is exactly what we are now

American Civil Liberties Union, "NSA Spying on Americans Is Illegal," December 29, 2005. Reproduced by permission.

witnessing in the case of the warrantless NSA [National Security Agency] spying ordered by President George W. Bush that was reported December 16, 2005 by the *New York Times*.

President Bush would sweep aside this entire body of democratically debated and painstakingly crafted restrictions on domestic surveillance by the executive branch.

According to the *Times*, Bush signed a presidential order in 2002 allowing the National Security Agency to monitor without a warrant the international (and sometimes domestic) telephone calls and e-mail messages of hundreds or thousands of citizens and legal residents inside the United States. The program eventually came to include some purely internal controls—but no requirement that warrants be obtained from the Foreign Intelligence Surveillance Court as the 4th Amendment to the Constitution and the foreign intelligence surveillance laws require.

In other words, no independent review or judicial oversight.

That kind of surveillance is illegal. Period.

The day after this shocking abuse of power became public, President Bush admitted that he had authorized it, but argued that he had the authority to do so. But the law governing government eavesdropping on American citizens is well-established and crystal clear. President Bush's claim that he is not bound by that law is simply astounding. It is a Presidential power grab that poses a challenge in the deepest sense to the integrity of the American system of government—the separation of powers between the legislative and executive branches, the concept of checks and balances on executive power, the notion that the president is subject to the law like everyone else, and the general respect for the "rule of law" on which our democratic system depends.

Flouting a Long History

The tensions between the need for intelligence agencies to protect the nation and the danger that they would become a domestic spy agency have been explicitly and repeatedly fought out in American history. The National Security Act of 1947 contained a specific ban on intelligence operatives from operating domestically. In the 1970s, America learned about the extensive domestic political spying carried out by the FBI, the military, the CIA, and the NSA, and Congress passed new laws to prevent a repeat of those abuses. Surveillance laws were debated and modified under presidents Gerald Ford, Jimmy Carter, Ronald Reagan, George Bush Sr. and Bill Clinton.

But, President Bush would sweep aside this entire body of democratically debated and painstakingly crafted restrictions on domestic surveillance by the executive branch with his extraordinary assertion that he can simply ignore this law because he is the Commander-in-Chief. In a December 17, 2005, radio address, for example, Bush asserted that the spying was "fully consistent with my constitutional responsibilities and authorities." But his constitutional duty is to "take care that the laws be faithfully executed" (Article II, Section 3); the law here clearly establishes well-defined procedures for eavesdropping on U.S. persons, and the fact is, Bush ordered that those procedures not be followed.

All electronic surveillance by the government in the United States is illegal, unless it falls under one of a small number of precise exceptions specifically carved out in law.

Government eavesdropping on Americans is an extremely serious matter; the ability to intrude on the private realm is a tremendous power that can be used to monitor, embarass, control, disgrace, or ruin an individual. Because it is so invasive, the technology of wiretapping has been subject to carefully crafted statutory controls almost since it was invented. Ignoring those controls and wiretapping without a court order is a crime that carries a significant prison sentence (in fact, criminal violations of the wiretap statute were among the articles of impeachment that were drafted against President Richard Nixon shortly before his resignation).

Clearly Illegal

Unfortunately, although the law in this matter is crystal clear, many Americans, faced with President Bush's bold assertions of "inherent" authority for these actions, will not know what to believe. There are only 5 points they need to understand:

Point #1: Electronic surveillance by the Government is strictly limited by the Constitution and Federal Law. The law on surveillance begins with the Fourth Amendment to the Constitution, which states clearly that Americans' privacy may not be invaded without a warrant based on probable cause.

United States Constitution: Fourth Amendment

The right of the people to be secure in their persons, houses, papers, and effects, against unreasonable searches and seizures, *shall not be violated*, and *no warrants shall issue, but upon probable cause*, supported by oath or affirmation, and particularly describing the place to be searched, and the persons or things to be seized. (emphasis added)

The U.S. Supreme Court (*U.S. v. Katz*) has made it clear that this core privacy protection does cover government eavesdropping. As a result, all electronic surveillance by the government in the United States is illegal, unless it falls under one of a small number of precise exceptions specifically carved out in the law.

United States Code Title 50, Chapter 36, Subchapter 1: Section 1809. Criminal sanction Prohibited activities

A person is guilty of an offense if he intentionally–

(1) engages in electronic surveillance under color of law except as authorized by statute

In other words, the NSA can only spy where it is explicitly granted permission to do so by statute. Citizens concerned about surveillance do not have to answer the question, "what law restricts the NSA's spying?" Rather, the government is required to supply an answer to the question "what law permits the NSA to spy?"

The Foreign Intelligence Surveillance Act is the law that governs eavesdropping on agents of 'foreign powers' within the United States, including suspected foreign terrorists.

The Only Three Laws That Permit Spying

Point #2: There are only three laws that permit the government to spy. There are only three laws that authorize any exceptions to the ban on electronic eavesdropping by the government. Congress has explicitly stated that these three laws are the exclusive means by which domestic electronic surveillance can be carried out (18 USC, Section 2511(2)(f)). They are:

- Title III and ECPA. Title III and the Electronic Communications Privacy Act make up the statutes that govern criminal wiretaps in the United States.

- FISA. The Foreign Intelligence Surveillance Act is the law that governs eavesdropping on agents of "foreign powers" within the United States, including suspected foreign terrorists.

Unauthorized Spying

Point #3: The Bush-NSA spying was not authorized by any of these laws. Title III and ECPA govern domestic criminal wiretaps and are not relevant to the NSA's spying. FISA is the law under which the NSA should have operated. It authorizes the government to conduct surveillance in certain situations without meeting all of the requirements of the Fourth Amendment that apply under criminal law, but requires that an independent Foreign Intelligence Surveillance Court oversee that surveillance to make sure that Americans who have no ties to foreign terrorist organizations or other "foreign powers" are not spied upon.

FISA was significantly loosened by the Patriot Act (which, for example, allowed it to be used for some criminal investigations), and parts of it now stand in clear violation of the Constitution's Fourth Amendment in the view of the ACLU [American Civil Liberties Union] and many others. However, even the post-Patriot Act version of FISA does not authorize the president to conduct warrantless eavesdropping on U.S. citizens or permanent legal residents in the U.S. without an order from the FISA Court. Yet it is that very court order requirement—imposed to protect innocent Americans—that the President has ignored.

In fact, one member of the FISA Court, Judge James Roberston, has apparently resigned from the court in protest of President Bush's secret authorization of this program. And the *New York Times* reported that the court's chief judge complained about the program when she was (belatedly) notified of it, and refused to allow information gathered under the program to be used as the basis for FISA wiretap orders.

NSA Spying Is Not Legitimate

Point #4: Congress's post-9/11 use-of-force resolution does not legitimize the Bush-NSA spying. Congress after 9/11 approved an Authorization to Use Military Force against those responsible for the attacks in order to authorize the president to conduct foreign military operations such as the invasion of Afghanistan.

But that resolution contains no language changing, overriding or repealing any laws passed by Congress. Congress does not repeal legislation through hints and innuendos, and the Authorization to Use Military Force does not authorize the president to violate the law against surveillance without a warrant any more than it authorizes him to carry out an armed robbery or seize control of Citibank in order to pay for operations against terrorists. In fact, when President Harry S. Truman tried to seize control of steel mills that were gripped by strikes in 1952, the Supreme Court decisively rejected his authority to make such a seizure, even in the face of arguments that the strike would interfere with the supply of weapons and ammunition to American troops then under fire on the battlefields of the Korean War.

U.S. Supreme Court: *Youngstown Co. v. Sawyer,* **343 U.S. 579 (1952)**

The order cannot properly be sustained as an exercise of the President's military power as Commander in Chief of the Armed Forces. . . .

Nor can the seizure order be sustained because of the several constitutional provisions that grant executive power to the President. . . . The Constitution limits his functions in the lawmaking process to the recommending of laws he thinks wise and the vetoing of laws he thinks bad. And the Constitution is neither silent nor equivocal about who shall make laws which the President is to execute. . . .

The Founders of this Nation entrusted the lawmaking power to the Congress alone in both good and bad times.

The Supreme Court also rejected similar assertions of inherent executive power by Richard Nixon.

In fact, FISA contains explicit language describing the president's powers "during time of war" and provides that "the President, through the Attorney General, may authorize electronic surveillance without a court order under this title to acquire foreign intelligence information *for a period not to exceed fifteen days following a declaration of war by the Congress.*" 50 U.S.C. § 1811 (emphasis added). So even if we accept the argument that the use-of-force resolution places us on a war footing, warrantless surveillance would have been legal for only 15 days after the resolution was passed on September 18, 2001.

Point #5: The need for quick action does not justify an end-run around the courts. The FISA law takes account of the need for emergency surveillance, and the need for quick action cannot be used as a rationale for going outside the law. FISA allows wiretapping without a court order in an emergency; the court must simply be notified within 72 hours. The government is aware of this emergency power and has used it repeatedly. In addition, the Foreign Intelligence court is physically located in the Justice Department building, and the FISA law requires that at least two of the FISA judges reside in the Washington, DC area, for precisely the reason that rapid action is sometimes needed.

If President Bush still for some reason finds these provisions to be inadequate, he must take his case to Congress and ask for the law to be changed, not simply ignore it.

The President Is Bound by the Rule of Law

President Bush's claim that he has "inherent authority" as Commander in Chief to use our spy agencies to eavesdrop on Americans is astonishing, and such spying is clearly illegal. It must be halted immediately, and its origins must be thoroughly investigated by Congress and by a special counsel.

Given the extensive (indeed, excessive) surveillance powers that the government already possesses, the Administration's blatantly illegal use of warrantless surveillance raises an important question: why? One possibility, raised by the *New York Times* in a Dec. 24, 2005 story ("Spy Agency Mined Vast Data Trove, Officials Report"), is that the NSA is relying on assistance from several unnamed telecommunications companies to "trace and analyze large volumes of communications" and is "much larger than the White House has acknowledged."

This, as security expert Bruce Schneier has noted, suggests the Bush Administration has developed a "a whole new surveillance paradigm"—exploiting the NSA's well-known capabilities to spy on individuals not one at a time, as FISA permits, but to run communications en masse through computers in the search for suspicious individuals or patterns. This "new paradigm" may well be connected to the NSA program sometimes known as "Echelon," which carries out just that kind of mass collection of communications. This "wholesale" surveillance, as Schneier calls it, would constitute an illegal invasion of Americans' privacy on a scale that has never before been seen.

The President of the United States has claimed a sweeping wartime power to brush aside the clear limits on his power set by our Constitution and laws.

According to the *Times*, several telecommunications companies provided the NSA with direct access to streams of communications over their networks. In other words, the NSA appears to have direct access to a large volume of Americans' communications—with not simply the assent, but the cooperation of the companies handling those communications.

We do not know from the report which companies are involved or precisely how or what the NSA can access. But this revelation raises questions about both the legal authority of the NSA to request and receive this data, and whether these companies may have violated either the Federal laws protecting these communications or their own stated privacy policies (which may, for example, provide that they will only turn over their customers' data with their consent or in response to a proper order).

Regardless of the scale of this spying, we are facing a historic moment: the President of the United States has claimed a sweeping wartime power to brush aside the clear limits on his power set by our Constitution and laws—a chilling assertion of presidential power that has not been seen since Richard Nixon.

7

The President's Surveillance Program Has Kept America Safe from Terrorists

George W. Bush

George W. Bush, former Republican governor of Texas, is the forty-third president of the United States.

The Patriot Act, passed by Congress after the devastating attacks of September 11, 2001, enables America's law enforcement personnel to investigate and prosecute terrorists and their supporters throughout the United States. The Authorization for Use of Military Force (AUMF), a joint resolution passed by Congress in September 2001, also gives the president the authority to fight the war on terrorism. Moreover, the Constitution obliges the president, as commander in chief of the U.S. armed forces, to lead the fight against America's enemies. The president, using the power given to him by the Patriot Act, the AUMF, and the U.S. Constitution, authorized the terrorist surveillance program to intercept international communications of people who have known links to al-Qaeda and other terrorist organizations. This program is a vital tool in the war against terror and has been critical in saving American lives.

As President, I took an oath to defend the Constitution, and I have no greater responsibility than to protect our people, our freedom, and our way of life. On September the 11th, 2001, our freedom and way of life came under attack by brutal enemies who killed nearly 3,000 innocent Americans.

George W. Bush, radio address to the American people, December 17, 2005.

We're fighting these enemies across the world. Yet in this first war of the 21st century, one of the most critical battlefronts is the home front. And since September the 11th, we've been on the offensive against the terrorists plotting within our borders.

One of the first actions we took to protect America after our nation was attacked was to ask Congress to pass the Patriot Act. The Patriot Act tore down the legal and bureaucratic wall that kept law enforcement and intelligence authorities from sharing vital information about terrorist threats. And the Patriot Act allowed federal investigators to pursue terrorists with tools they already used against other criminals. Congress passed this law with a large, bipartisan majority, including a vote of 98-1 in the United States Senate.

Since then, America's law enforcement personnel have used this critical law to prosecute terrorist operatives and supporters, and to break up terrorist cells in New York, Oregon, Virginia, California, Texas and Ohio. The Patriot Act has accomplished exactly what it was designed to do: it has protected American liberty and saved American lives.

Yet key provisions of this law are set to expire [on December 31, 2005]. The terrorist threat to our country will not expire [on that date.] The terrorists want to attack America again, and inflict even greater damage than they did on September the 11th. Congress has a responsibility to ensure that law enforcement and intelligence officials have the tools they need to protect the American people.

The House of Representatives passed reauthorization of the Patriot Act. Yet a minority of senators filibustered to block the renewal of the Patriot Act when it came up for a vote. That decision is irresponsible, and it endangers the lives of our citizens. The senators who are filibustering must stop their delaying tactics, and the Senate must vote to reauthorize the Patriot Act. In the war on terror, we cannot afford to be without this law for a single moment.

Presidential Authority

To fight the war on terror, I am using authority vested in me by Congress, including the Joint Authorization for Use of Military Force, which passed overwhelmingly in the first week after September the 11th. I'm also using constitutional authority vested in me as Commander-in-Chief.

In the weeks following the terrorist attacks on our nation, I authorized the National Security Agency, consistent with U.S. law and the Constitution, to intercept the international communications of people with known links to al Qaeda and related terrorist organizations. Before we intercept these communications, the government must have information that establishes a clear link to these terrorist networks.

The activities conducted under this authorization have helped detect and prevent possible terrorist attacks in the United States and abroad.

This is a highly classified program that is crucial to our national security. Its purpose is to detect and prevent terrorist attacks against the United States, our friends and allies. Yesterday the existence of this secret program was revealed in media reports, after being improperly provided to news organizations. As a result, our enemies have learned information they should not have, and the unauthorized disclosure of this effort damages our national security and puts our citizens at risk. Revealing classified information is illegal, alerts our enemies, and endangers our country.

As the 9/11 Commission pointed out, it was clear that terrorists inside the United States were communicating with terrorists abroad before the September the 11th attacks, and the commission criticized our nation's inability to uncover links between terrorists here at home and terrorists abroad. Two of the terrorist hijackers who flew a jet into the Pentagon, Nawaf al Hamzi and Khalid al Mihdhar, communicated while they were in the United States to other members of al Qaeda who were overseas. But we didn't know they were here, until it was too late.

The authorization I gave the National Security Agency after September the 11th helped address that problem in a way that is fully consistent with my constitutional responsibilities and authorities. The activities I have authorized make it more likely that killers like these 9/11 hijackers will be identified and located in time. And the activities conducted under this authorization have helped detect and prevent possible terrorist attacks in the United States and abroad.

The activities I authorized are reviewed approximately every 45 days. Each review is based on a fresh intelligence assessment of terrorist threats to the continuity of our government and the threat of catastrophic damage to our homeland. During each assessment, previous activities under the authorization are reviewed. The review includes approval by our nation's top legal officials, including the Attorney General and the Counsel to the President. I have reauthorized this program more than 30 times since the September the 11th attacks, and I intend to do so for as long as our nation faces a continuing threat from al Qaeda and related groups.

This authorization is a vital tool in our war against the terrorists.

The NSA's activities under this authorization are thoroughly reviewed by the Justice Department and NSA's top legal officials, including NSA's general counsel and inspector general. Leaders in Congress have been briefed more than a dozen times on this authorization and the activities conducted under it. Intelligence officials involved in this activity also receive extensive training to ensure they perform their duties consistent with the letter and intent of the authorization.

A Vital Tool

This authorization is a vital tool in our war against the terrorists. It is critical to saving American lives. The American people expect me to do everything in my power under our laws and Constitution to protect them and their civil liberties. And that is exactly what I will continue to do, so long as I'm the President of the United States.

8

The President's Surveillance Program Threatens All Americans' Civil Rights

Bob Barr

Bob Barr is an attorney and a Republican member of the House of Representatives from Georgia from 1995–2003.

The president's order to conduct electronic surveillance on American citizens and residents without a warrant is contrary to American law. The Constitution—and American courts—does not permit the president to break the law in the name of national security. The resolution passed by Congress authorizing the use of military force does not include the provision that the president can override federal laws governing electronic surveillance. Nor does the U.S. Supreme Court permit electronic surveillance without a warrant, even in the event of protecting national security. If the president does not like the law concerning electronic surveillance, then he should ask Congress to change it via legal legislative processes.

Back in the 1930s, when confronted with clear evidence he had violated the law, Georgia's then-agriculture commissioner and gubernatorial candidate Eugene Talmadge popped his bright red suspenders and dared those accusing him of corruption to do something about it, declaring, "Sure, I stole, but I stole for you." He was elected Governor in 1932. Accused of breaking the law in the current debate over electronic spying, President George W. Bush has, in his own way, dared the American people to do something about it. For the sake of our Constitution, I hope they will.

Let's focus briefly on what the President has done here. Exactly like Nixon before him, Bush has ordered the National Security Agency (NSA) to conduct electronic snooping on communications of various people, including U.S. citizens. That action is unequivocally contrary to the express and implied requirements of federal law that such surveillance of U.S. persons inside the U.S. (regardless of whether their communications are going abroad) must be preceded by a court order. General Michael Hayden, a former director of the NSA and now second in command at the new Directorate of National Intelligence, testified to precisely that point at a congressional hearing in April 2000. In response, the President and his defenders have fallen back on the same rationale used by Nixon, saying essentially, "I am the Commander in Chief; I am responsible for the security of this country; the people expect me to do this; and I am going to do it." But the Supreme Court slapped Nixon's hands when he made the same point in 1972. And it slapped Bush's hands when, after 9/11, he asserted authority to indefinitely detain those he unilaterally deemed "enemy combatants"—without any court access.

Bush's advocates also argue that the congressional resolution authorizing military force in Afghanistan and elsewhere—to bring to justice those responsible for the 9/11 attacks—authorized those no-warrant wiretaps. But there is absolutely nothing in the clear language of that resolution or in its legislative history suggesting that it was intended to override specific federal laws governing electronic surveillance. If Bush succeeds in establishing this as a precedent, he will have accomplished a breathtaking expansion of unilateral Executive power that could be easily applied to virtually any other area of domestic activity as long as a link to national security is asserted.

Finally, presidential defenders have argued that efficiency demands bypassing the courts. There again, the clear language of the law does them in. Even pre–Patriot Act law provided a very robust mechanism through which a President, facing what he believes is such an emergency that the short time needed to secure court approval for a wiretap would obviate the need for one, can order a tap without prior court approval as long as he eventually gets an O.K. within three days. If that degree of flexibility does not suit a President, it is hard to imagine what provision would. And if the President thought the law governing eavesdropping was misguided or impractical, he should have proposed amendments.

Tomorrow, it may be your phone calls or e-mails that will be swept up into our electronic infrastructure and secretly kept in a growing file attached to your name.

Today Alleged Terrorists, Tomorrow All Citizens?

The Supreme Court has unanimously rejected the assertion that a President may conduct electronic surveillance without judicial approval for national security, noting in 1972 that our "Fourth Amendment freedoms cannot properly be guaranteed if domestic security surveillances may be conducted solely within the discretion of the Executive Branch." Rather than abiding such a clear missive, the Administration instead is taking the road mapped out nearly two centuries ago by Andrew Jackson, who, in response to a Supreme Court decision he didn't like, ignored it and is said to have declared, "The Supreme Court has made its decision. Now let them enforce it."

Alleged associates of al-Qaeda are today's targets of that breathtaking assertion of presidential power. Tomorrow, it may be your phone calls or e-mails that will be swept up into our electronic infrastructure and secretly kept in a growing file attached to your name. Then everyone you contact could become a suspect, a link in an ever lengthening chain that would ensnare us all in the files of the largest database ever created through unlimited electronic spying that touches every aspect of our lives.

9

The President Has the Authority to Identify and Detain Enemy Combatants

Clarence Thomas

Clarence Thomas is an associate justice on the U.S. Supreme Court, appointed by President George H.W. Bush in 1991.

The president has the constitutional authority and responsibility to protect America's national security. He is therefore completely within his legal rights and war powers to detain a prisoner captured on a battlefield as an enemy combatant. Judicial interference in the issue of whether or not the detainee is in fact an enemy results in second-guessing the president and can be harmful to national security, as the courts may lack important information known only to the president.

The Executive Branch, acting pursuant to the powers vested in the President by the Constitution and with explicit congressional approval, has determined that Yaser Hamdi is an enemy combatant and should be detained. This detention falls squarely within the Federal Government's war powers, and we lack the expertise and capacity to second-guess that decision. . . .

"It is 'obvious and unarguable' that no governmental interest is more compelling than the security of the Nation." *Haig v. Agee*, (1981) (quoting *Aptheker v. Secretary of State*, (1964)). The national security, after all, is the primary responsibility and purpose of the Federal Government. . . . But because the

Clarence Thomas, dissenting opinion, *Hamdi vs. Rumsfeld*, 542 U.S. 507 (2004).

Founders understood that they could not foresee the myriad potential threats to national security that might later arise, they chose to create a Federal Government that necessarily possesses sufficient power to handle any threat to the security of the Nation. [Alexander Hamilton wrote in *The Federalist No. 23* that] the power to protect the Nation

> "ought to exist without limitation ... *[b]ecause it is impossible to foresee or define the extent and variety of national exigencies, or the correspondent extent & variety of the means which may be necessary to satisfy them.* The circumstances that endanger the safety of nations are infinite; and for this reason no constitutional shackles can wisely be imposed on the power to which the care of it is committed."

The President Must Protect National Security

The Founders intended that the President have primary responsibility—along with the necessary power—to protect the national security and to conduct the Nation's foreign relations. They did so principally because the structural advantages of a unitary Executive are essential in these domains. . . .

Congress, to be sure, has a substantial and essential role in both foreign affairs and national security. But it is crucial to recognize that *judicial* interference in these domains destroys the purpose of vesting primary responsibility in a unitary Executive. I cannot improve on Justice [Robert H.] Jackson's words, speaking for the Court:

> The President, both as Commander-in-Chief and as the Nation's organ for foreign affairs, has available intelligence services whose reports are not and ought not to be published to the world. It would be intolerable that courts, without the relevant information, should review and perhaps nullify actions of the Executive taken on information properly held secret. Nor can courts sit *in camera* in order to be taken into executive confidences. But even if courts

could require full disclosure, the very nature of executive decisions as to foreign policy is political, not judicial. Such decisions are wholly confided by our Constitution to the political departments of the government, Executive and Legislative. They are delicate, complex, and involve large elements of prophecy. They are and should be undertaken only by those directly responsible to the people whose welfare they advance or imperil. They are decisions of a kind for which the Judiciary has neither aptitude, facilities nor responsibility and which has long been held to belong in the domain of political power not subject to judicial intrusion or inquiry.

The Courts Should Not Second-guess the President

Several points, made forcefully by Justice Jackson, are worth emphasizing. First, with respect to certain decisions relating to national security and foreign affairs, the courts simply lack the relevant information and expertise to second-guess determinations made by the President based on information properly withheld. Second, even if the courts could compel the Executive to produce the necessary information, such decisions are simply not amenable to judicial determination because "[t]hey are delicate, complex, and involve large elements of prophecy." Third, the Court in *Chicago & Southern Air Lines* and elsewhere has correctly recognized the primacy of the political branches in the foreign-affairs and national-security contexts.

We lack the information and expertise to question whether [an individual] is actually an enemy combatant, a question the resolution of which is committed to other branches.

For these institutional reasons and because "Congress cannot anticipate and legislate with regard to every possible action the President may find it necessary to take or every possible situation in which he might act," it should come as no surprise that "[s]uch failure of Congress ... does not, 'especially ... in the areas of foreign policy and national security,' imply 'congressional disapproval' of action taken by the Executive." Rather, in these domains, the fact that Congress has provided the President with broad authorities does not imply—and the Judicial Branch should not infer—that Congress intended to deprive him of particular powers not specifically enumerated. . . .

Finally, . . . where "the President acts pursuant to an express or implied authorization from Congress, he exercises not only his powers but also those delegated by Congress[, and i]n such a case the executive action 'would be supported by the strongest of presumptions and the widest latitude of judicial interpretation, and the burden of persuasion would rest heavily upon any who might attack it.'" That is why the Court has explained, in a case analogous to this one, that "the detention[,] ordered by the President in the declared exercise of his powers as Commander in Chief of the Army in time of war and of grave public danger[, is] not to be set aside by the courts without the clear conviction that [it is] in conflict with the Constitution or laws of Congress constitutionally enacted."
. . .

I acknowledge that the question whether Hamdi's executive detention is lawful is a question properly resolved by the Judicial Branch, though the question comes to the Court with the strongest presumptions in favor of the Government. The plurality agrees that Hamdi's detention is lawful if he is an enemy combatant. But the question whether Hamdi is actually an enemy combatant is "of a kind for which the Judiciary has neither aptitude, facilities nor responsibility and which has long been held to belong in the domain of political power not subject to judicial intrusion or inquiry." *Chicago & Southern Air Lines.* That is, although it is appropriate for the Court to determine the judicial question whether the President has the asserted authority, we lack the information and expertise to question whether Hamdi is actually an enemy combatant, a question the resolution of which is committed to other branches. . . .

The Due Process Clause Permits Detention

Due process requires nothing more than a good-faith executive determination. To be clear: The Court has held that an executive, acting pursuant to statutory and constitutional authority may, consistent with the Due Process Clause, unilaterally decide to detain an individual if the executive deems this necessary for the public safety *even if he is mistaken*. . . .

The Executive's decision that a detention is necessary to protect the public need not and should not be subjected to judicial second-guessing.

In *Luther v. Borden*, (1849), the Court discussed the President's constitutional and statutory authority, in response to a request from a state legislature or executive, "'to call forth such number of the militia of any other State or States, as may be applied for, as he may judge sufficient to suppress [an] insurrection.'" The Court explained that courts could not review the President's decision to recognize one of the competing legislatures or executives. If a court could second-guess this determination, "it would become the duty of the court (provided it came to the conclusion that the President had decided incorrectly) to discharge those who were arrested or detained by the troops in the service of the United States." "If the judicial power extends so far," the Court concluded, "the guarantee contained in the Constitution of the United States [referring to Art. IV, §4] is a guarantee of anarchy, and not of order." The Court clearly contemplated that the President had authority to detain as he deemed necessary, and such detentions evidently comported with the Due Process Clause as long as the President correctly decided to call forth the militia, a question the Court said it could not review.

The Court also addressed the natural concern that placing "this power in the President is dangerous to liberty, and may be abused." The Court noted that "[a]ll power may be abused if placed in unworthy hands," and explained that "it would be difficult . . . to point out any other hands in which this power would be more safe, and at the same time equally effectual." Putting that aside, the Court emphasized that this power "is conferred upon him by the Constitution and laws of the United States, and must therefore be respected and enforced in its judicial tribunals." Finally, the Court explained that if the President abused this power "it would be in the power of Congress to apply the proper remedy. But the courts must administer the law as they find it." . . .

The Government's asserted authority to detain an individual that the President has determined to be an enemy combatant, at least while hostilities continue, comports with the Due Process Clause. As these cases also show, the Executive's decision that a detention is necessary to protect the public need not and should not be subjected to judicial second-guessing. Indeed, at least in the context of enemy-combatant determinations, this would defeat the unity, secrecy, and dispatch that the Founders believed to be so important to the warmaking function.

Accordingly, I conclude that the Government's detention of Hamdi as an enemy combatant does not violate the Constitution. By detaining Hamdi, the President, in the prosecution of a war and authorized by Congress, has acted well within his authority. Hamdi thereby received all the process to which he was due under the circumstances. I therefore believe that this is no occasion to balance the competing interests, as the plurality unconvincingly attempts to do. . . .

I realize that many military operations are, in some sense, necessary. But many, if not most, are merely expedient, and I see no principled distinction between the military operation the plurality condemns today (the holding of an enemy combatant based on the process given Hamdi) from a variety of other military operations. In truth, I doubt that there is any sensible, bright-line distinction. It could be argued that bombings and missile strikes are an inherent part of war, and as long as our forces do not violate the laws of war, it is of no constitutional moment that civilians might be killed. But this does not serve to distinguish this case because it is also consistent with the laws of war to detain enemy combatants exactly as the Government has detained Hamdi. This, in fact, bolsters my argument . . . to the extent that the laws of war show that the power to detain is part of a sovereign's war powers.

Undeniably, Hamdi has been deprived of a serious interest, one actually protected by the Due Process Clause. Against this, however, is the Government's overriding interest in protecting the Nation. If a deprivation of liberty can be justified by the need to protect a town, the protection of the Nation, *a fortiori*, justifies it.

10

The President Does Not Have the Authority to Detain Enemy Combatants

Timothy Lynch

Attorney Timothy Lynch is the director of the Project on Criminal Justice and the associate director of the Center for Constitutional Studies of the Cato Institute, a libertarian public-policy research foundation based in Washington, D.C.

The writ of habeas corpus ensures that a prisoner literally has his day in court to hear and contest the charges against him. The Constitution allows the president to suspend the writ, but only in cases of rebellion or invasion. The government's argument that courts may not "second-guess" the president's determination that a prisoner is an enemy combatant is specious, since the whole purpose of habeas corpus is to determine if the government's decision to detain a prisoner is rightfully held. Since the president has not suspended the writ in the case of Hamdi vs. Rumsfeld, *the prisoner and his attorney must be allowed to appear in court to argue his case that he is being held unlawfully.*

The petitioner, Yaser Esam Hamdi, is an American citizen. He is presently confined in a military brig in the United States. A petition for a writ of habeas corpus has been filed on his behalf and that petition alleges that Mr. Hamdi's imprisonment is contrary to the law.

Timothy Lynch, amicus curiae brief to the Supreme Court, *Hamdi vs. Rumsfeld*, 542 U.S. 507 (2004), Washington, DC: Cato Institute. Reproduced by permission.

The Government claims that Mr. Hamdi is an "enemy combatant"—a soldier affiliated with the Taliban, the former government of Afghanistan. Mr. Hamdi appears to have been initially seized by the Northern Alliance forces in Afghanistan and he was thereafter turned over to the U.S. military. Mr. Hamdi was then transferred to a U.S. military base in Cuba where prisoners from the war in Afghanistan are being held. In April 2002, the Government moved Mr. Hamdi to a naval brig in Norfolk, Virginia.

For almost two years, the Government has denied Mr. Hamdi any access to legal counsel. The Government claims that the Executive has unilateral authority to identify "enemy combatants" and to hold them incommunicado indefinitely. Because it is physically impossible for a prisoner to file a writ of habeas corpus in such circumstances, an attorney must file a "next friend" petition on the prisoner's behalf. The Government's position is that such petitions must be "properly filed" even though the attorney has not been able to meet with the prisoner to discuss the Government's allegations. The Government also maintains that properly filed petitions should be summarily dismissed if the prisoner has been deemed by the executive authorities to be an "enemy combatant."

The Government is using the 'enemy combatant' label to revive [the] claim that when the country is at war, the president becomes 'the supreme legislator, supreme judge, and supreme executive.'

The Government's Sweeping Claims

Since the September 11th terrorists attacks, the Federal Government has made several sweeping constitutional claims— that the Executive can seize American citizens, place them in solitary confinement, deny any and all visitation (including with legal counsel), and, in effect, deny the prisoner access to Article III judges to seek the habeas "discharge" remedy. As long as the Executive has issued "enemy combatant" orders to his Secretary of Defense, the Government claims, the process comports with the Constitution—regardless of whether the prisoner is an American citizen or whether the arrest-seizure takes place overseas or on American territory. Repeatedly, the Government conflates three distinct issues: seizure of citizens, detention of citizens, and trial of citizens. In effect, the Government is using the "enemy combatant" label to revive Attorney General James Speed's claim that when the country is at war, the president becomes "the supreme legislator, supreme judge, and supreme executive." *Ex Parte Milligan*, (1866). This Court should reject that claim in the most emphatic terms. . . .

The Constitution provides that "The Privilege of the Writ of Habeas Corpus shall not be suspended, unless when in Cases of Rebellion or Invasion the public Safety may require it." Clearly, the Constitution contemplates exigent circumstances in which "public Safety" will require the Executive to move swiftly against persons who are perceived to be dangerous. In those situations, it is likely that the Executive will not be able to comply with constitutional norms for every search, arrest, and imprisonment. The suspension of the writ will thus excuse otherwise illegal arrests and dragnet tactics because emergency circumstances can warrant such actions.

As long as the writ of habeas corpus is *not* suspended, however, the Executive must follow constitutional norms.

Thus far, the resolution of this case is straightforward and uncomplicated. If the writ of habeas corpus has not been suspended, it retains its full legal force. The prisoner here, Mr. Hamdi, is an American citizen and the petition that has been filed on his behalf complains that his confinement is unlawful. The startling fact that Mr. Hamdi has not been able to meet with an attorney to fully present a habeas petition appears to be plain error. The Government, however, denies the force of this contention. Having conceded the major premise—that the writ has not been suspended—the Government challenges the minor premise—that the writ retains its full legal force. On the Government's view, the Constitution requires improvised habeas procedures for "enemy combatants."

The Government advances two arguments to support this theory. The first argument is that Article III courts may not "second-guess" the Executive's "enemy combatant" determination—even in habeas corpus petitions that have been properly filed on behalf of American citizens. That shocking assertion strikes at the heart of habeas corpus.

The right to habeas corpus is, in essence, a right to judicial protection against lawless incarceration by executive authorities.

The "Great Writ"

The right to habeas corpus is, in essence, a right to judicial protection against lawless incarceration by executive authorities. If the judiciary could not "second-guess" and reject the Executive's initial decision to imprison a citizen, the writ would never have acquired its long-standing reputation in the law as the "Great Writ." By way of background, here is how Justice Story defined the writ in his treatise on constitutional law:

> *Habeas Corpus*, literally, Have you the Body. The phrase designates the most emphatic words of the writ, issued by a Judge or Court, commanding a person, who has another in custody, or in imprisonment, to have his body (Habeas Corpus) before the Judge or Court, at a particular time and place, and to state the cause of his imprisonment. The person, whether a sheriff, gaoler, or other person, is bound to produce the body of the prisoner at the time and place appointed; and, if the prisoner is illegally or improperly in custody, the Judge or Court will discharge him. Hence it is deemed the great security of the personal liberty of the citizen against oppression and illegal confinement.

Justice Story was hardly alone in holding that the writ was a "great security" for individual liberty. The writ was widely lauded on both sides of the Atlantic. William Blackstone, for example, said the writ of habeas corpus was "the most celebrated writ in English law."

Although the judiciary may not "second-guess" the Executive when the writ of habeas corpus has been suspended, this Court should firmly reject the Government's attempt to get around habeas review by employing the "enemy combatant" designation against citizens. The law of habeas corpus cannot be so easily evaded.

The Government's second argument is simply a variation of the first, and is basically a fall-back position. The claim is that Article III courts can "only require the military to point to some evidence supporting *its* [enemy combatant] determination." (Emphasis in original). The "evidence" means nothing in the context of habeas review if an Article III judge has no authority to examine it. The Government attempts to justify this improvised habeas procedure because this case involves the conduct of agents who report to the Executive's Secretary of Defense, not the Executive's Attorney General. This argument must also fail. "The writ of habeas corpus is the fundamental instrument for safeguarding individual freedom against arbitrary and lawless state action. . . . The very nature of the writ demands that it be administered with the initiative and flexibility to insure that miscarriages of justice within its reach are surfaced and corrected." *Harris v. Nelson*, (1969). In the words of Justice Holmes, "habeas corpus cuts through all forms." . . .

The *Territo* Case

The Government is correct in arguing that—an American citizen who chooses to join enemy forces and fight against the U.S. military must live with the consequences of that decision. Such a person can be killed on the battlefield or, should he surrender, be taken into custody as a prisoner of war. Since the privilege of citizenship does not immunize a person from such battlefield captures, such persons need not be indicted with formal criminal charges. While a treason prosecution is certainly a possibility, such persons may also be detained as POWs [prisoners of war].

The case of Gaetano Territo is instructive. See *In re Territo*, (1946). Mr. Territo was serving in the Italian Army during World War II when he was taken prisoner by the U.S. Army. After his capture, he was transferred from a prison facility in Italy to a prison facility on American soil. At some point after his arrival in the U.S., Mr. Territo filed a petition for a writ of habeas corpus. The gravamen of his petition was that, because he had been born in the U.S., his imprisonment on American soil, without formal criminal charges, was contrary to law.

The U.S. military, the Department of Justice, and the federal courts treated Mr. Territo's legal petition with respect. There was no dispute over the prisoner's access to counsel. And there was no dispute regarding the interplay between the Executive's power to seize persons and the Court's power to review the legality of such seizures. Mr. Territo was able to meet with an attorney, and his legal counsel was able to present his grievance to an impartial Article III judge. The Government was, of course, afforded an opportunity to explain the circumstances of Mr. Territo's capture, and to argue that his confinement was lawful and appropriate.

After due consideration, both the district court and the appellate court agreed with the Government that citizenship does not alter "the status of one captured on the field of battle." Mr. Territo's petition for a writ of habeas corpus was thus properly considered and sensibly denied.

The petition that is at issue in this case was dismissed too casually. The prisoner, Mr. Hamdi, has not been heard from. . . .

The prisoner must be allowed to consult with his attorney in a private setting. An evidentiary hearing should then be held and the prisoner should have an opportunity to address the Court, and his counsel must have an opportunity to rebut the Government's allegations at the hearing. As in *Territo*, the Government should, of course, be given an opportunity to defend the legality of its actions. If the Government can persuade an Article III judge that this detention is lawful and proper, Mr. Hamdi should be remanded to the military brig. If the Government is unable to persuade an Article III judge that this detention is lawful and proper, it has three options: (a) initiate criminal proceedings (where the full panoply of constitutional protections will be afforded the prisoner); (b) initiate deportation proceedings; or (c) release the prisoner from custody.

Ex Parte Quirin Ruling Does Not Involve Detention

Because this appeal concerns the law of habeas corpus and the Executive's power to hold a citizen incommunicado, the Government's ubiquitous references to *Ex Parte Quirin* (1942) are plainly inapposite.

The *Quirin* ruling involved prosecution and trial procedures, not detention. And the single most important legal matter to note about *Quirin* is this: *The prisoners in that case did not contest their status as "enemy combatants."* In truth, the *Quirin* ruling does not extend to any situation in which a prisoner *contests* the Government's "enemy combatant" allegation. Despite the sweeping representations of the Government in its various filings, the precedential value of *Quirin* has been, and will continue to be, limited to its facts.

Ex Parte Milligan Bolsters Right to Trial by Jury

The right to trial by jury is guaranteed in explicit terms by the Sixth Amendment and is further bolstered by this Court's ruling in *Ex Parte Milligan*, In *Milligan*, this Court recognized that even when the writ of habeas corpus is suspended, the Executive does not acquire the power to prosecute and execute prisoners. Rather, the suspension of the writ merely expands the power of the Executive to detain persons who are perceived to be dangerous.

To be sure, the Government retains the prerogative to revive the unpersuasive arguments that were advanced by Attorney General Speed in his losing bid in the *Milligan* litigation, but such a course of action should be pursued openly and forthrightly. Unfortunately, the Government, in its zeal to change the law, has been mistating the law as it presently stands. Repeatedly, the Government invokes the *Quirin* ruling to conflate three distinct issues: seizure, detention, and prosecution. *Quirin* has no bearing on seizure and detention. And, to the extent that it deals with prosecution and trial procedure, it only applies to prisoners who do not contest their status as "enemy combatants."

11

The President May Authorize Torture to Protect National Security

John Yoo

John Yoo is a law professor at the University of California, Berkeley, and a former deputy assistant attorney general in the Justice Department's Office of Legal Counsel under President George W. Bush.

The Geneva Conventions, the primary international agreement detailing how prisoners of war must be treated in regard to food, shelter, clothing, health care, and religion, do not apply in the war on terror. The terrorist organization al-Qaeda is not a nation-state, as the Geneva Conventions define enemies at war, and the Taliban militia in Afghanistan has lost its right to have its members treated as POWs since the militia members do not wear uniforms and consistently violate accepted conventions of warfare. While detainee members of these groups housed in the United States are nevertheless treated humanely according to the convention's provisions, the president's power as commander in chief includes the authority to interrogate captured terrorists as he sees fit to obtain information vital to protecting the safety of American citizens.

Official Washington has been struck by a paroxysm of leaking. It involves classified memos analyzing how the Geneva Convention, the 1994 Torture Convention and a fed-

John Yoo, "With All Necessary and Appropriate Force," *Los Angeles Times*, June 11, 2004. Reproduced by permission.

eral law banning torture apply to captured Al Qaeda and Taliban fighters. Critics suggest that the Bush administration sought to undermine or evade these laws. Sen. Dianne Feinstein (D-Calif.) claimed ... that the analyses appeared "to be an effort to redefine torture and narrow prohibitions against it."

The Geneva Convention and Terrorists

This is mistaken. As a matter of policy, our nation has established a standard of treatment for captured terrorists. In February 2002, President George W. Bush declared that the detainees held at Guantanamo Bay, Cuba, would be treated "humanely and, to the extent appropriate and consistent with military necessity, consistent with the principles" of the Geneva Convention. Detainees receive shelter, food, clothing, healthcare and the right to worship.

This policy is more generous than required. The Geneva Convention does not apply to the war on terrorism. It applies only to conflicts between its signatory nations. Al Qaeda is not a nation; it has not signed the convention; it shows no desire to obey the rules. Its very purpose—inflicting civilian casualties through surprise attack—violates the core principle of laws of war to spare innocent civilians and limit fighting to armed forces. Although the convention applies to the Afghanistan conflict, the Taliban militia lost its right to prisoner-of-war status because it did not wear uniforms, did not operate under responsible commanders and systematically violated the laws of war.

It is true that the definition of torture in the memos is narrow, but that follows the choice of Congress. When the Senate approved the international Torture Convention, it defined torture as an act "specifically intended to inflict severe physical or mental pain or suffering." It defined mental pain or suffering as "prolonged mental harm" caused by threats of physical harm or death to a detainee or a third person, the administration of mind-altering drugs or other procedures "calculated to disrupt profoundly the senses or the personality." Congress adopted that narrow definition in the 1994 law against torture committed abroad, but it refused to implement another prohibition in the convention—against "cruel, inhuman or degrading treatment or punishment"—because it was thought to be vague and undefined.

In the war on terrorism, Congress has authorized the president to use 'all necessary and appropriate force.'

Physical and mental abuse is clearly illegal. But would limiting a captured terrorist to six hours' sleep, isolating him, interrogating him for several hours or requiring him to do physical labor constitute "severe physical or mental pain or suffering"? Federal law commands that Al Qaeda and Taliban operatives not be tortured, and the president has ordered that they be treated humanely, but the U.S. is not required to treat captured terrorists as if they were guests at a hotel or suspects held at an American police station.

Finally, critics allege that the administration wants to evade these laws by relying on the president's commander-in-chief power. But the 1994 statute isn't being evaded, because the president's policy is to treat the detainees humanely. Besides, that statute does not explicitly regulate the president or the military. General criminal laws are usually not interpreted to apply to either, because otherwise they could interfere with the president's constitutional responsibility to manage wartime operations. If laws against murder or property destruction applied to the military in wartime, for instance, it could not engage in the violence that is a necessary part of war.

But suppose Congress did specifically intend to restrict the president's authority to interrogate captured terrorists. As commander in chief, the president still bears the responsibility to wage war. To this day, presidents from both political parties have refused to acknowledge the legality of the War Powers Resolution, which requires congressional approval for hostilities of more than 60 days. (President Clinton ignored it during Kosovo.) And in the war on terrorism, Congress has authorized the president to use "all necessary and appropriate force."

By exploring the boundaries of what is lawful, the administration's analyses identified how a decision maker could act in an extraordinary situation. For example, suppose that the United States captures a high-level Al Qaeda leader who knows the location of a nuclear weapon in an American city. Congress should not prevent the president from taking necessary measures to elicit its location, just as it should not prohibit him from making other strategic or tactical choices in war. In hearings Sen. Charles E. Schumer (D-N.Y.) recognized that "very few people in this room or in America . . . would say that torture should never, ever be used, particularly if thousands of lives are at stake."

Ultimately, the administration's policy is consistent with the law. If the American people disagree with that policy, they have options: Congress can change the law, or the electorate can change the administration.

12

The President Does Not Have the Authority to Permit Torture

Andrew Sullivan

Andrew Sullivan is a columnist and former editor for the New Republic.

The president has systematically taken advantage of the practice of issuing signing statements to put his own spin on the laws he signs. An important example of this presidential overreaching is his interpretation of the McCain amendment of December 2005—a law that bans all "cruel, inhuman, and degrading" treatment of detainees in U.S. military prisons. The president believes that if he thinks torturing a detainee is warranted, he is justified in ignoring the law and authorizing the torture. While the president has the right to act on his own to protect the country, he can not exempt himself from the laws that govern his country. The United States is a democracy, not a monarchy.

A somewhat legal law is a little like a somewhat pregnant woman. At first blush, it seems like an absurdity. But President Bush disagrees. In the past five years, quietly but systematically, he has been arguing that the law doesn't always apply to him. How has he done this? By attaching "signing statements" that spell out his own attitude to bills he signs.

Previous Presidents have sporadically issued signing statements, but seldom and mainly as boilerplate or spin. Until the

1980s, there had been just over a dozen in two centuries. The President's basic legislative weapon, after all, is the veto power given him by the founders. He can use the power as leverage to affect legislation or kill it. But he cannot legislate himself or interpret the law counter to Congress's intent. Signing statements were therefore relatively rare instances of presidential nuance or push-back. In eight years, Ronald Reagan used signing statements to challenge 71 legislative provisions, and Bill Clinton 105.

In five years, President Bush has already challenged up to 500 provisions, according to one tally—far, far more than any predecessor. But more important than the number under Bush has been the systematic use of the statements and the scope of their content, asserting a very broad legal loophole for the Executive. Last December [2005] for example, after a year of debate, the President signed the McCain amendment into law. In the wake of Abu Ghraib, the amendment banned all "cruel, inhuman and degrading" treatment of U.S. military detainees. For months, the President threatened a veto. Then the Senate passed it 90 to 9. The House chimed in with a veto-proof majority. So Bush backed down, embraced McCain and signed it. The debate was over, right? That's how our democracy works, right?

Not according to this President. Although the meaning of the law was crystal clear and the Constitution says Congress has the exclusive power to "make Rules concerning Captures on Land and Water," Bush demurred.

He issued a signing statement that read, "The executive branch shall construe Title X in Division A of the Act, relating to detainees, in a manner consistent with the constitutional authority of the President to supervise the unitary executive branch and as Commander in Chief and consistent with the constitutional limitations on the judicial power."

Translation: If the President believes torture is warranted to protect the country, he'll violate the law and authorize torture. If the courts try to stop him, he'll ignore them too. This wasn't quibbling or spinning. Like the old English kings who insisted that Parliament could not tell them what to do, Bush all but declared himself above a law he signed. One professor who specializes in this constitutional area, Phillip J. Cooper of Portland State University in Oregon, has described the power grabs as "breathtaking."

A Democracy cannot work if the person who is deputed to execute the laws exempts himself from them when he feels like it.

And who came up with this innovative use of presidential signing statements? Drumroll, please. Samuel Alito, Supreme Court nominee, way back in 1986. In a Feb. 5 memo, he wrote, "Since the president's approval is just as important as that of the House or Senate, it seems to follow that the president's understanding of the bill should be just as important as that of Congress." That is, of course, a very strange idea—which is why, until then, signing statements had been sporadic and rare. Courts have always looked solely to congressional debates in interpreting laws Congress has passed. In laws with veto-proof margins, the President's view is utterly irrelevant. Alito seemed to concede that at the time, recognizing the "novelty of the procedure and the potential increase of presidential power."

Alito, of course, didn't foresee the war on terrorism. But put a war President's power together with the new use of signing statements, and Executive clout has been put on steroids. "If you take this to its logical conclusion, because during war the Commander in Chief has an obligation to protect us, any statute on the books could be summarily waived," argued Senator Lindsey Graham, a Republican from South Carolina.

As Graham shows, this isn't a Republican-Democrat issue. It's a very basic one. A President, Democrat or Republican, has every right to act unilaterally at times to defend the country. But a democracy cannot work if the person who is deputed to execute the laws exempts himself from them when he feels like it. Forget the imperial presidency. This is more like a monarchical one. America began by rejecting the claims of one King George. It's disturbing to think we may now be quietly installing a second one.

Organizations to Contact

The editors have compiled the following list of organizations concerned with the issues debated in this book. The descriptions are derived from materials provided by the organizations. All have publications or information available for interested readers. The list was compiled on the date of publication of the present volume; names, addresses, and phone numbers may change. Be aware that many organizations take several weeks or longer to respond to inquiries, so allow as much time as possible.

American Alliance for Rights and Responsibilities (AARR)
1725 K St. NW, Suite. 1112, Washington, DC   20006
(202) 785-7844 • fax: (202) 785-4370

AARR believes that democracy can work only if the defense of individual rights is matched by a commitment to individual and social responsibility. It is dedicated to restoring the balance between rights and responsibilities in American life. It publishes the bimonthly newsletter *Rights and Responsibilities*.

American Civil Liberties Union (ACLU)
125 Broad St., 18th Floor., New York, NY   10004
(212) 549-2500 • fax: (212) 549-2646
Web site: www.aclu.org

The ACLU is a national organization that works to defend Americans' civil rights as guaranteed by the U.S. Constitution. It provides legal defense, research, and education. Among the ACLU's numerous publications are "In Defense of Freedom in a Time of Crisis," "Bigger Monster, Weaker Chains: The Growth of an American Surveillance Society," and "Civil Liberties After 9-11: The ACLU Defends Freedom."

American Enterprise Institute (AEI)
1150 17th St. NW, Washington, DC   20036

(202) 862-5800 • fax: (202) 862-7177
Web site: www.aei.org

The American Enterprise Institute for Public Policy Research is a scholarly research institute dedicated to preserving limited government, private enterprise, and a strong foreign policy and national defense. It publishes the books *Democratic Realism: An American Foreign Policy for a Unipolar World* and *Study of Revenge: The First World Trade Center Attack* and *Saddam Hussein's War Against America.* Articles about executive power can be found in its magazine, *American Enterprise,* and on its Web site.

The Brookings Institution
1775 Massachusetts Ave. NW, Washington, DC   20036
(202) 797-6000 • fax: (202) 797-6004
e-mail: brookinfo@brook.cdu
Web site: www.brookings.org

The institution, founded in 1927, is a think tank that conducts research and education in foreign policy, economics, government, and the social sciences. In 2001 it created America's Response to Terrorism, a project that provides briefings and analysis to the public and which is featured on the center's Web site. The site also offers transcripts from conferences entitled "Executive Power and Due Process: Supreme Court Rules on 'Enemy Combatants'" and "Detention and Interrogation of Captured 'Enemies': Do Law and National Security Clash?" Among its publications are the study "Rights, Liberties, and Security: Recalibrating the Balance After September 11," the quarterly *Brookings Review,* and periodic *Policy Briefs.*

Cato Institute
1000 Massachusetts Ave. NW, Washington, DC   20001
(202) 842-0200 • fax: (202) 842-3490
e-mail: cato@cato.org
Web site: www.cato.org

The institute is a libertarian public policy research foundation dedicated to limiting the role of government and protecting individual liberties. It publishes the quarterly magazine *Regu-*

lation, the bimonthly *Cato Policy Report*, and numerous policy papers and articles. Works on presidential powers include "The Imperial Presidency and the War on Terror" and "Wartime Executive Power and the NSA's Surveillance Authority II."

Center for Defense Information
1779 Massachusetts Ave. NW, Suite. 615
Washington, DC 20036
(202) 332-0600 • fax: (202) 462-4559
e-mail: info@cdi.org
Web site: www.cdi.org

The center is a nonpartisan, nonprofit organization that researches all aspects of global security. It seeks to educate the public and policy makers about issues such as security strategies and terrorism. It publishes the monthly publication *Defense Monitor* and the book *Imperial America: A Double-Barreled Attack on American War Policy*.

Central Intelligence Agency (CIA)
Office of Public Affairs, Washington, DC 20505
(703) 482-0623 • fax: (703) 482-1739
Web site: www.cia.gov

The CIA, created in 1947 by President Harry S. Truman, is responsible for collecting—openly and secretly—information about foreign governments, corporations, and individuals who may pose a threat to the safety of the United States. The agency is also charged with analyzing and reporting its findings to various other agencies of the government. Publications, including *Factbook on Intelligence*, are available on its Web site.

Common Cause
1250 Connecticut Ave. NW, Suite. 600
Washington, DC 20036
(202) 833-1200
Web site: www.commoncause.org

Common Cause is a liberal lobbying organization that works to improve the ethical standards of Congress and government in general. Its priorities include campaign reform, making government officials accountable for their actions, and promoting civil rights for all citizens. Common Cause publishes the quarterly *Common Cause Magazine* as well as position papers and reports.

Federal Bureau of Investigation (FBI)
935 Pennsylvania Ave. NW, Room 7972
Washington, DC   20535
(202) 324-3000
Web site: www.fbi.gov

The mission of the FBI is to uphold the law through the investigation of violations of federal criminal law; to protect the United States from foreign intelligence and terrorist activities; to provide leadership and law enforcement assistance to federal, state, local, and international agencies; and to perform these responsibilities in a manner that is responsive to the needs of the public and is faithful to the U.S. Constitution. Press releases, congressional statements, and major speeches on issues concerning the FBI are available on the agency's Web site, as are the fact sheet *The Use and Purpose of National Security Letters* and the report *The FBI's Counterterrorism Program Since September 2001*.

The Heritage Foundation
214 Massachusetts Ave. NE, Washington, DC   20002
(202) 546-4400 • fax: (202) 546-0904
e-mail: info@heritage.org
Web site: www.heritage.org

The foundation is a conservative public policy research institute dedicated to free-market principles, individual liberty, and limited government. Its resident scholars publish position papers on a wide range of issues in its *Backgrounder* series and in its quarterly journal *Policy Review*. Available on its Web site are the articles "The Use and Abuse of Executive Orders and Other Presidential Directives" and "Domestic Surveillance: Dual Priorities, National Security and Civil Liberties Must Be Met."

National Security Agency
9800 Savage Rd., Ft. Meade, MD   20755-6248
(301) 688-6524
e-mail: nsapao@nsa.gov
Web site: www.nsa.gov

The agency coordinates, directs, and performs activities, such as designing cipher systems, that protect American information systems and produce foreign intelligence information. It is the largest employer of mathematicians in the United States and also hires the nation's best codemakers and codebreakers. Speeches, briefings, and reports are available at the Web site.

People for the American Way (PFAW)
2000 M St. NW, Suite. 400, Washington, DC   20036
(202) 467-4999 • fax: (202) 293-2672
e-mail: pfaw@pfaw.org
Web site: www.pfaw.org

PFAW works to increase tolerance and respect for America's diverse cultures, religions, and values such as freedom of expression. It distributes educational materials, leaflets, and brochures and publishes the quarterly *Press Clips*, a collection of newspaper articles concerning censorship. Available on its Web site is the memo "Senate Caves on Wiretapping Issue, Continues Erosion of Checks and Balances," and "Illegal NSA Spying Program: Myths and Facts."

Progressive Policy Institute (PPI)
600 Pennsylvania Ave. SE, Suite. 400, Washington, DC   20003
(202) 546-0007 • fax: (202) 544-5014
Web site: www.dlcppi.org

PPI is a public policy research organization that strives to develop alternatives to the traditional debate between liberals and conservatives. It advocates economic policies designed to stimulate broad upward mobility and social policies designed to liberate the poor from poverty and dependence on government support. The institute publishes the articles "Bring Gitmo Under the Rule of Law" and "Cyber Tools for Countering Terrorism."

RAND Corporation
1700 Main St., PO Box 2138, Santa Monica, CA 90407-2138
(310) 393-0411 • fax: (310) 393-4818
Web site: www.rand.org

RAND is an independent, nonprofit research and advisory organization on issues of national security and the public welfare. It is funded by federal, state, and local governments and by private foundations and other philanthropic sources. Its publications include the commentaries "Strike a Balance by Weighing Threats" and "President Obscured the Case for Spying."

Bibliography

Books

James Bamford   *Body of Secrets: Anatomy of the Ultra-Secret National Security Agency.* New York: Anchor, 2002.

Peter Berkowitz, ed.   *Terrorism, the Laws of War, and the Constitution: Debating the Enemy Combatant Cases.* Stanford, CA: Hoover Institution Press, 2005.

Phillip J. Cooper   *By Order of the President: The Use and Abuse of Executive Direct Action.* Lawrence: University Press of Kansas, 2002.

Louis Fisher   *Military Tribunals and Presidential Power: American Revolution to the War on Terror.* Lawrence: University Press of Kansas, 2005.

Louis Fisher   *Presidential War Power.* 2nd rev. ed. Lawrence: University Press of Kansas, 2004.

Peter Irons   *War Powers: How the Imperial Presidency Hijacked the Constitution.* New York: Metropolitan, 2005.

Anatol Lieven   *America Right or Wrong: An Anatomy of American Nationalism.* New York: Oxford University Press, 2004.

Kenneth R. Mayer *With the Stroke of a Pen: Executive Orders and Presidential Power.* Princeton, NJ: Princeton University Press, 2001.

James Risen *State of War: The Secret History of the C.I.A. and the Bush Administration.* New York: Free Press, 2006.

Mark J. Rozell *Executive Privilege: Presidential Power, Secrecy, and Accountability.* 2nd rev. ed. Lawrence: University Press of Kansas, 2002.

Andrew Rudalevige *The New Imperial Presidency: Renewing Presidential Power After Watergate.* Ann Arbor: University of Michigan Press, 2005.

Mark Tushnet, ed. *The Constitution in Wartime: Beyond Alarmism and Complacency.* Raleigh, NC: Duke University Press, 2005.

John Yoo *The Powers of War and Peace: The Constitution and Foreign Affairs after 9/11.* Chicago: University of Chicago Press, 2005.

Periodicals

Vladimir Buikovsky "Torture's Long Shadow," *Washington Post*, December 18, 2005.

Debra Burlingame "Our Right to Security," *Wall Street Journal*, January 30, 2006.

James Carafano, Todd Gaziano, and Alane Kochems	"Domestic Surveillance: Dual Priorities, National Security, and Civil Liberties," Heritage Foundation Web Memo #950, December 21, 2005. www.heritage.org/research/homelanddefense/wm950.cfm.
Center for Security	"Too Little Surveillance?" Center for Security Policy Decision Policy Brief No. 06-D 07, February 6, 2006. www.centerforsecurityPolicy.org/index.jsp?section=papers&code=06-D_07.
Morgan Cloud	"The Bugs in Our System," *New York Times*, January 13, 2006.
David Cole	"NSA Spying Myths," *Nation*, February 20, 2006.
Jackson Diehl	"Inhuman: Yes or No?" *Washington Post*, September 12, 2005.
Viet D. Dinh	"Detentions Are Appropriate," *USA Today*, December 19, 2004.
Richard A. Epstein	"Executive Power on Steroids," *Wall Street Journal*, February 13, 2006.
Barton Gellman and Dafna Linzer	"Pushing the Limits of Wartime Powers," *Washington Post*, December 18, 2005.
Michael S. Greco	"It's Time to Restore the Balance," *ABA News*, December 20, 2005.
Gene Healy	"Jose Padilla: Constitutional Unperson?" *Miami Herald*, September 24, 2005.

Charles Hurt	"Carter Allowed Surveillance in 1977," *Washington Times*, February 11, 2006.
Charles Hurt	"'Warrantless' Searches Not Unprecedented," *Washington Times*, December 22, 2005.
Ron Hutcheson	"Like Some Predecessors, Bush Asserts Broad Powers in Time of War," *Grand Forks (ND) Herald*, December 22, 2005.
J. Bradley Jansen	"Warrantless Searches or Constitutional Protections?" EnterStageRight.com, May 27, 2002. www.enterstageright.com/archive/articles/0502/0502mailsearch.htm.
Charles Krauthammer	"How Do You Think We Catch the Bad Guys?" *Time*, January 16, 2006.
Edward Lazarus	"Warrantless Wiretapping: Why It Seriously Imperils the Separation of Powers, and Continues the Executive's Sapping of Power from Congress and the Courts," FindLaw.com, December 22, 2005. http://writ.findlaw.com/lazarus/20051222.html.
David Luban	"Torture, American-Style," *Washington Post*, November 27, 2005.
Andrew McCarthy	"Warrantless Searches of Americans? That's Shocking!" *National Review Online*, December 20, 2005.

New York Times   "Excerpts from Arguments Before Supreme Court on Detention of U.S. Citizens," April 29, 2004.

Paul Rosenzweig   "Balancing Liberty and Security," Heritage Foundation Commentary, May 14, 2003. www.heritage.org/ Press/Commentary/ed051403a.cfm.

Paul Rosenzweig   "Don't Put Security at Risk," *USA Today*, June 28, 2004.

Charlie Savage   "Bush Challenges Hundreds of Laws," *Boston Globe*, April 30, 2006.

Jonathan Schell   "The Hidden State Steps Forward," *Nation*, January 9, 2006.

John Schmidt   "President Had Legal Authority to OK Taps," *Chicago Tribune*, December 21, 2005.

Jeffrey H. Smith   "Central Torture Agency?" *Washington Post*, November 9, 2005.

Stuart Taylor Jr.   "Rights, Liberties, and Security: Recalibrating the Balance After September 11," *Brookings Review*, Winter 2003.

Joe Thompson   "Bush Wiretapping Program Scary, Flunks Legality Test," *Houston Chronicle*, February 5, 2006.

Washington Post   "Director for Torture," November 23, 2005.

Washington Post   "Torture and the Constitution," December 11, 2005.

John C. Yoo   "The President's Constitutional Authority to Conduct Military Operations Against Terrorists and Nations Supporting Them," U.S. Department of Justice, Office of Legal Counsel memorandum, September 25, 2001. www.usdoj.gov/olc/ warpowers925.htm.

Web Sites

Executive Branch Resources (www.gpoaccess.gov/executive .html). The Government Printing Office maintains this comprehensive archive. Student researchers can instantly locate up-to-date records on the regulatory process (implementing laws passed by Congress), presidential materials (remarks, speeches, and executive orders), and executive publications (reports, investigations, and other findings).

Presidents of the United States (www.presidentsusa.net). This comprehensive research site, sponsored by CB Presidential Research Services, includes the useful link "Powers and Limitations," offering information from constitutional provisions, statutory language, executive orders, and the War Powers Act; historical analysis of presidential acts; and critical examination of the proper exercise of executive power.

Index